I  S

Illegal Immigration—An Unfolding Crisis

Daniel James

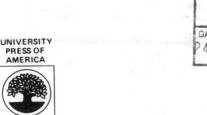

UNIVERSITY
PRESS OF
AMERICA

Lanham • New York • London

Mexico-United States Institute
Washington, D.C.

Copyright © 1991 by Daniel James

University Press of America®, Inc.
4720 Boston Way
Lanham, Maryland 20706

3 Henrietta Street
London WC2E 8LU England

Co-published by arrangement with
The Mexico-United States Institute

Library of Congress Cataloging-in-Publication Data

James, Daniel.
Illegal immigration : an unfolding crisis / by Daniel James.
p.   cm.
Includes bibliographical references.
1. Alien labor, Mexican—United States.
2. Aliens, Illegal—United States.   I. Title.
HD8081.M6J36   1991
325' .272073—dc20   91-24879 CIP

ISBN 0-8191-8404-7 (hardback, alk. paper)
ISBN 0-8191-8405-5 (pbk., alk. paper)

The paper used in this publication meets the minimum requirements of
American National Standard for Information Sciences—Permanence
of Paper for Printed Library Materials, ANSI Z39.48–1984.

Contents

Tables

Preface

IF WE THINK of "immigration" as simply the movement of human beings from one place to another, it becomes clear that the often vexing phenomenon of immigration in our time is as old as humanity itself. Our earliest ancestors were perpetual "immigrants," moving about constantly in search of food and shelter or to flee predators or inhospitable environments. Those who founded this country were perhaps unique among the immigrants of all time—with the possible exception of the Hebrews Moses led out of Egypt—in that they were motivated not by material concerns but by an ideal: freedom. Our founders became the first human beings to build a society predicated upon the philosophical premise that everyone was created equal—a premise that is as moral as it is idealistic.

Why, then, do we pass laws intended to restrict our society only to those whom we select to share it with us? Why should immigration—that is, the movement of people from place to place—not be as free and unfettered as it once was? These are complex questions which will be debated as long as human beings, clustered in groups of their own kind, jealously mark out as their own a given patch of land—conditioned, that is, by what Robert Ardrey called the "territorial imperative." Such larger questions are, however, beyond the purview of this study.

We are not concerned here, for example, with the issue of how much immigration America should or can absorb in the future. The subject of our study is narrower, though obviously it cannot be divorced from the problem of immigration as a whole. It is confined to an examination of illegal immigration, involving people who enter the United States "without inspection"—that is, without proper documentation—and their ever growing impact upon American society.

The impact of illegal immigration upon our society is already considerable, as the study documents. It affects almost every aspect of our lives, from the neighborhoods we live in to the jobs we seek, and raises questions about the very stability of America if measures are not taken to control it. The development of a foreign underclass is one of the potentially explosive social forces that massive illegal immigration produces, with its implications of non-assimilable ethnic enclaves and unlawful acts in association with criminal elements including drug traffickers.

The study makes clear that, in general, the increasing numbers who resort to illegal means to enter the United States do so not with the intention of violating our laws; they are law-abiding people who are motivated to leave their country—Mexico, in most cases—only because they desperately seek decent jobs, food, shelter, and security. Mexico is unable to fulfill those needs largely because it has been experiencing a profound crisis which has yet to run its course. The administration of President Carlos Salinas de Gortari is making valiant efforts to resolve the crisis, but until that happens the United States can expect an increasing number of Mexicans to enter its territory without acquiring the proper documentation. Immigration experts cited in the study estimate that the trend will continue into the next century.

Although this study concerns illegal immigration, it has been impossible to explore all aspects of the problem. Thus the experiences of the Haitian and Cuban "boat people," important as they are, are not treated because the study focuses on Mexico as the greatest source, by far, of illegal immigration into the United States. We can only hope that this will be but the beginning of an ongoing project, the aim of which would be to study further a rapidly unfolding national crisis.

Acknowledgements

THE FIELD of immigration research is relatively new, but the body of work already in existence is astonishingly large and continues to grow. Without it, the author would have found the going much harder than it was. He therefore acknowledges, first and foremost, his indebtedness to the scholars and researchers who have made a substantial contribution to an understanding of the problem.

Among those who were most helpful in providing valuable information and insight were James McLean and Denise Blackburn of the U.S. Immigration and Naturalization Service, Ira Mehlman of the American Federation for Immigration Reform, Rob Paral of the National Association of Latino Elected and Appointed Officials, Ambassador Philip Sánchez, the National Council of La Raza, the Bureau of the Census, the General Accounting Office, and the Department of State. Phillip N. Truluck, Executive Vice President of the Heritage Foundation, made important suggestions in the course of reviewing the first draft of the study.

The author wishes to acknowledge, most especially, the indispensable assistance of Rebecca de Malo, Program Director of the Mexico-United States Institute, who contributed greatly to both the editing process and the production of camera-ready copy, embellished by attractive stylistic innovations. Last but not least, our administrative assistant, Polly Goodman, deserves mention for carrying some of the burden of research and proofing while also handling an often hectic office schedule.

This study is the first to be published by the Mexico-United States Institute; others, not necessarily on the same subject, are planned for later publication. The Institute, however, bears no responsibility for the opinions, views, or statements contained therein. They are solely the author's responsibility.

1

The Rising Influx of Illegal Immigrants

WE WANT ORDER ON OUR BORDER

Those words, emblazoned on red bumper stickers on hundreds of cars parked along the U.S. border opposite Tijuana, bluntly express the resentment of American residents over nightly incursions into their area of swarms of illegal Mexican immigrants. From 1989 to the present, passenger autos and pickups converge there at night with headlights turned on to maximum brightness, creating a blinding glare visible on the Mexican side of the narrow strip of marshland ahead. This "Light Up the Border" campaign at the Otay Mesa crossing, near San Diego, was organized by a U.S. Border Patrol agent's widow and the city's former mayor to protest rising illegal immigration. It has partially achieved its objective of convincing the U.S. Government to install stadium lighting in the Tijuana River levee area, which deters illegal entries there; but they have increased in adjacent border areas.[1]

Farther north, in Washington, D.C., a group calling itself the Coalition for Freedom organized a seminar on illegal immigration entitled "The Sinister Invasion." The speakers were highly respected academics and former officials of the Immigration and Naturalization Service and Customs Service, sophisticated professionals who would never dream of demonstrating at the border. But their message was substantially the same as that of the "Light Up the Border" people: Unremitting illegal immigration was sowing disorder along the 2,000-mile stretch separating Mexico and the United States.

Though not directly related but attesting to the volatility of the border these days, in the same month of the Otay Mesa protest,

1

November 1990, some residents of Mexicali, on the other side of the line well to the east of Tijuana, staged a protest against the killing of a 16-year-old Mexican allegedly by a U.S. Border Patrol agent. They succeeded in closing the border for nine hours, making it impossible for legal migrants to report for work on farms in Southern California's Imperial Valley.

Jorge Bustamante, a leading Mexican immigration expert who heads the College of the Northern Border, a think tank based in Tijuana and Ciudad Juárez which specializes in immigration problems, ridiculed the "Light Up the Border" protesters. He charged them with hypocrisy. "This thing of losing control of the border is a kind of joke," he declared. "They don't want to have control of the border. It would be uneconomic."[2] Mexican workers cross illegally into the United States, he explained, because of the big demand there for cheap labor.

In California itself, counter demonstrations by Hispanic and immigrant advocacies were organized, their leaders accusing the border protesters of "racism." One counter protest was held by the Friends Service Committee's U.S.-Mexico Border Program in San Diego, which denounced the anti-illegals movement co-led by the city's own former mayor. Some pro-illegal activists went so far as to charge the Border Patrol with indiscriminately killing persons who try to cross into the United States without proper documentation.

The illegal entry of human beings into the United States, overwhelmingly from Mexico, is an issue that is potentially as explosive as the illegal traffic in narcotics. It is a persistent irritant that could severely damage relations between the two neighbors. In fact, both problems are intertwined: the Department of Justice has reported a significant rise in both drug smuggling and illegal immigration during 1990 and into 1991. This grim dual trend may be a harbinger of what the last decade of the 20th century might bring.

The illegal movement of both drugs and human beings is frequently accompanied by violence. Besides the killing in Mexicali, 14 other Mexicans were shot to death along the border in 1990, and many others were wounded by gunfire. Nine of them were killed by border bandits and "*coyotes*," Mexican smugglers who prey on the illegals. Four of the remaining six deaths, including that of the Mexicali youth, were charged by immigrant advocacies to the Border

Patrol. A "badlands atmosphere in an area overwhelmed by illegal immigration and drug trafficking," is how the Southern California border is described in a *Washington Post* account citing U.S. authorities.[3]

"This last [agricultural] season the violence has increased a lot, and it worries us a lot," the *Post* story goes on to quote Luis Wybo Alfaro, Director General of Border Affairs in the Mexican Government's Department of Foreign Relations.[4]

As illegal immigration has rebounded, the problems and social tensions it brings have correspondingly multiplied. Cross-border drug violations shot up in 1990 and California National Guardsmen and U.S. Marines had to pitch in to help the INS, Customs Service, and Drug Enforcement Administration to monitor the border. Marines had traded gunfire with illegal alien drugrunners the year before.

Navy Seabees have fortified fencing along the most heavily transitted segment of the border, the San Diego Sector, where smugglers of aliens and drugs have made a practice of simply driving their wards into the United States through gaps in border fences. In 1989, the INS and the International Boundary and Water Commission proposed to dig a ten-mile drainage ditch in western San Diego County that would also serve to block illegal cross-border auto and truck traffic. The proposal was shelved in the face of a chorus of protests from immigrant and civil rights advocates.

U.S. border communities are feeling increasingly beleaguered by the housing blight, crime, education and welfare burdens, and in general the disruption that have accompanied the resurgence of illegal immigration. Overcrowding has become the most common of many housing code violations in immigrant-impacted areas of Los Angeles. A 1987 *Los Angeles Times* survey concluded that as many as 200,000 people were living illegally in converted garages.[5]

All four Southwest border states, but particularly Texas, share a relatively new problem: *colonias* — shantytowns, heavily populated by illegals and possessing only minimal water and sanitary facilities.[6] The rapid growth of the colonias, already overcrowded with a population of 400,000 which is expected to double in a few years, has sparked pressures for new outlays of Federal and state funds to ameliorate their Third World-like lot. Some opponents have cautioned that publicly financed improvements would only reward the slumlords and encourage further proliferation.

Owners of well-kept, carefully zoned housing developments in Encinitas, San Diego County, have found that increasingly their neighborhoods are invaded by illegal alien squatters who inhabit tents or caves. Other residents of once serene border neighborhoods complain of a growing procession of illegals in their streets and backyards, with acts of crime (not necessarily committed by them) following not far behind. Among other consequences, the Los Angeles Unified School District found it must plan for a 20 percent annual rise in its operating costs to educate alien children. The State of California saw the cost of Medicaid for indigent illegal aliens* reach $300 million in 1990.

Signs of serious federal action to halt rising border violations are at best uncertain. Legislation on legal-immigration reform (PL 101-649), enacted late in 1990, made deportation easier, raised the penalties for document fraud, and provided for 1,000 more Border Patrol agents (based on assumed future appropriations). But dropped at the last moment was a proposed pilot project to curb immigration document fraud by improving the reliability of state drivers licenses.[7] On the other hand, major Hispanic advocacies decided to make their top legislative priority for the 102nd Congress the repeal of employer sanctions, which they consider profoundly discriminatory against Hispanics.

***

Americans know it as the "Soccer Field," a plain covering two acres opposite Tijuana south of San Diego. For Mexicans, it is "Zapata Canyon"—an odd rubric, since Emiliano Zapata, the revolutionary peasant general after whom it might have been named, hailed

---

*Some immigration analysts interchange this term with "undocumented immigrant" or "unauthorized immigrant," but the U.S. Immigration and Naturalization Service prefers the term, "illegal alien." One whose visa has expired is not "undocumented" or "unauthorized," while legal residents or citizens do not need to be "documented"; but foreigners who enter the country without documentation are aliens who are here illegally. To avoid repetition, we shall interchange freely "alien" with "immigrant" while prefixing either one with the adjective "illegal" or "illicit."

from a region south of Mexico City very far away. Though it lies in U.S. territory, it is the chief staging area for prospective illegal immigrants from Mexico. When night falls, most of the Mexican men, women, and children who have congregated in Zapata Canyon head north through the mesas and ravines, hoping to rejoin loved ones in the United States, to find jobs, or both.** Some bring in contraband or prey on targets of opportunity, including their fellow illegal aliens.

Observing the nightly massing of humanity at the Soccer Field, a handful of U.S. Border Patrol agents will intercept some of them and, after perfunctory paperwork, send them back to Mexico. No sooner do they arrive, however, than many will head back to El Norte again. As the numbers have grown and the aliens themselves have become more assertive, so have the risks of patrolling the border. A total of 363 Border Patrol agents were the targets of assaults in 1990 — the highest number ever — with weapons varying from knives to stones to guns. Most nights, more than a thousand border crossers, some of them women with babes in arms, will elude the Border Patrol and melt into the huge illegal population of the United States.

Illegal immigration is on the rise again. After a period of decline, it is once more moving upward coincident with a decade of economic stagnation and rapid population growth in Mexico: 1990 showed a 20 percent jump over 1989, and arrests of illegal Mexicans broke the one million mark for the first time since 1987. All other indicators of increasing illegal immigration also leaped ahead in

---

**The sight of a group of poor immigrants huddled together in the cold dark night of Zapata Canyon wrenches the heart of anyone who has witnessed it for the first time, as I did some years ago. I was accompanying a Border Patrol agent on his rounds when an order crackled over his radio to hasten to intercept them and to rendezvous with another agent at the appointed spot. What had been ghostly silhouettes on the horizon, as seen through an infrared night-vision sensor scope, materialized suddenly under unsparing headlights as human beings with panic written on their bronzed faces.

Addressing them in Spanish, I learned that they had trudged here on foot from as far south as Oaxaca, a distance of perhaps 1,200 miles. Oaxaca is much closer to Mexico's southern neighbor, Guatemala, only about 350 miles away, but none of this group would ever have dreamed of going there. They knew that they would find in Guatemala only the same grinding poverty they had left in their own country. It was *El Norte* they were eager to reach — the land of milk and honey north of Mexico. The oldest of them, a wizened woman with stooped shoulders and of indeterminate age — prototypically she was probably fortyish but looked sixty or over — was as desirous of beginning a new life among the northern strangers as was a lad who told me he was fourteen. They were too paralyzed with fear to give much more information to an inquisitive *gringo*.

1990: arrests of alien smugglers up 37 percent; seizures of smugglers' vehicles, 63.2 percent; the value of narcotics seized by the Border Patrol, 32 percent (to an incredible $1.6 billion).[8] Best estimates are that the predominantly Mexican illegal population of the United States, despite 3 million legalizations since 1987, today totals between 3 and 5 million and is growing by about 300,000 a year.

INS apprehensions of illegal aliens, at best a crude measure of total illegal border crossings, reached an all-time high of 1.7 million in 1986. When Congress, late that year, passed the Immigration Reform and Control Act (IRCA)—which penalized employers of illegal aliens, boosted Border Patrol strength, and screened illegals from welfare rolls—apprehensions dropped 30 percent. There was hope that the new law would finally close the "back door" of illegal immigration. By 1989, arrests of illegal aliens were down 44 percent from the 1986 peak. Visa overstayers also dropped in number.

The amnesty of more than three million former illegal aliens accounted for much of the decrease. Aliens who were legalized could enter and leave the United States freely, and no longer appeared in INS apprehension statistics.

Most of the 1,000 new positions that Congress voted for the Border Patrol—a 28 percent increase—fell victim to budget austerity. Only 3,857 of the nation's 4,324 Border Patrol agents are now assigned to guard our long border with Mexico. Of these, only about 800 are on duty at any one time. Moreover, as Senator Dennis DeConcini (D.-AZ) has repeatedly pointed out, "the amount of time spent [by the Border Patrol] on border enforcement activities along the Southwest border has declined 11 percent."[9]

The centerpiece of IRCA, the reform law, was supposed to be employer sanctions, a way of turning off the magnet of jobs that lure illegal aliens to the United States. But the deterrent effect of employer sanctions has withered under the proliferation of false ID documents—more bitter fruit of illegal immigration.

"We've been seeing the apprehension numbers going up, and at the same time, we've been seeing more and more people carrying fraudulent documents," was how the problem was put by Dale Musegades, Chief Border Patrol Agent in the El Paso area, as reported in the *New York Times*. He added wryly, "And the quality of the documents has been improving."[10]

Counterfeiters apprehended in Harlingen, Texas, in late 1990, had employed a laser scanning device to produce near perfect copies of ID documents such as Social Security cards. The market for documents of that kind is enormous, as indicated by the seizure in Houston, in January 1990, of a single cache of 25,000 counterfeit ID documents. As Agent Musegades summed it up: "They have adapted to employer sanctions and found a way around it."[11]

***

Ironically, these ugly trends manifest themselves at a time when Mexico and the United States appear to be moving ever closer together in the fields of trade and economic interchange, and in general seem to be enjoying an era of cordial relations which is unprecedented in recent decades. Both President George Bush and Mexico's President Carlos Salinas de Gortari have repeatedly demonstrated, in word and deed, that they are profoundly committed to making the new cordial binational relationship permanent. They even speak of a future in which the economies of the two neighbors will be integrated. Yet lurking in the shadows is the potential for serious friction as illegal immigration mounts steadily and causes many vexing problems.

Equally, or perhaps more alarming, is not only the potential for friction between the two neighbors inherent in the illegals problem but also among important segments of our own society. Americans themselves are divided over the issue, as we saw above, whether on ethnic, political, humanitarian, or legal grounds. This can be a two-edged sword. On the one hand, as the Hispanic population of the southwestern states grows apace — in California, our biggest state, it increased from 19.2 percent to 25.8 percent of the total population between 1980 and 1990, according to the 1990 Census[12]—it is bound to elect its own people to important local, state, and national offices and they might well raise a nationwide hue and cry on behalf of the illegals. On the other hand, a surprisingly large number of U.S. citizens of Mexican origin, particularly in Texas, are strongly opposed to permitting illegal immigrants into the country under most circumstances. Thus the U.S. Hispanic community itself is divided.

Disagreement among "Anglos" on how to deal with the illegals issue is, if anything, sharper yet. Besides the "Light Up the Border" movement, irate Americans, including lawmakers, have at various times called for the "militarization of the border" to halt the illegals influx. Others would erect concrete walls to keep them out. At the other extreme, groups such as the Friends Service Committee and American Civil Liberties Union oppose any steps that may deprive illegals of their "rights." They take the position that there is nothing basically illegal about crossing a border in search of work.

Unless a solution satisfactory to all parties concerned is reached soon, not only could bilateral relations suffer a severe setback but U.S. society as a whole could become torn by schisms. The Southwest is particularly susceptible, due to the exponential rise in its Hispanic population of predominantly Mexican origin, but major northern states are not much less vulnerable. In New York, for example, the Hispanic population increased by an astonishing 33.4 percent between 1980 and 1990.[13] Now second to the blacks as the state's biggest minority, it could conceivably overtake them if black growth remains about where it is—15.9 percent—as projected, while Hispanics grow at the present or a higher rate. The likelihood is that Hispanics will again leap forward in number by the year 2000, as a result of the continued "push" from south of the border and their high rate of population growth.

The problem will probably become acute in the remaining years of this century and first years of the next, for the trend is toward a decided increase in the flow of Mexicans into this country illegally. Three million or more illegals, the great majority of them Mexicans, are expected to enter during the 1990s—and that is a conservative estimate, since more than one million of them were apprehended in 1990 alone. A still larger number of Mexicans is likely to cross the border illegally between 2000 and 2010.[14] The Mexican illegal movement will probably be augmented by hundreds of thousands of persons from Central America, thus swelling the grand total of illegal aliens to numbers that are impossible to project. If, for example, economic and political conditions in their countries should deteriorate further, the number of Mexicans and Central Americans compelled under those circumstances to cross into the United States illegally could reach the proportions of a human tidal wave.

The presence of swelling millions of illegal aliens in the United States who cannot be assimilated in the short run could pose, eventually, a threat to its stability and security. Although this problem may well develop into the most important one Americans will have to face in the next generation, the country at large seems scarcely aware of it. The Administration, apart from those agencies directly involved such as INS, has shown little interest in it judging by its policies and statements; it is obsessed, rather, by the problems of countries far from these shores. Likewise our nation's lawmakers, excepting perhaps those from the border states, seem more concerned about other issues, whether foreign or domestic, than the illegals problem. Even when our leaders focus on such crucial matters as the President's program for revitalizing education, and they dwell upon how much it will cost and who will pay for it, few factor into their discussion the additional burden illegals represent for many school districts. It is as if a "conspiracy of silence" existed about the problem of illegals in our midst.

Yet they already constitute a threat to our very sovereignty. For if, by definition, the movement of people from one nation to another without the latter's consent is a violation of its fundamental laws, that constitutes a breach of its sovereignty. The 159 members of the United Nations recognize that every sovereign nation-state has the right to guard and protect its borders, and the right, above all, to determine who shall be permitted to enter and reside within its national territory.

Illegal immigration could have all sorts of social and political consequences. One of the most important is its negative impact upon the labor market in certain urban areas, where the presence of a large number of illegal aliens willing and able to work for much less than the average legal worker tends to depress wages. Even immigrants who have arrived legally can be affected: A U.S. Department of Labor study finds, for example, that a 10 percent increase in the number of new immigrants willing to work decreases the average wage of foreign-born workers by between 2 and 3 percent.[15]

A dangerous side effect of the illegal immigration is that it tends to create a foreign underclass. Persons who do not have proper documentation live in fear of detection by the authorities and of resultant imprisonment or deportation to their homelands. It is to protect themselves that they resort to false identification papers, including Social Security cards and drivers licenses, thus compounding their violation of the law, and worse, nurturing the vast industry in counterfeit documents of all kinds noted above. Fear of detection makes them pliable victims of unscrupulous employers as well as unscrupulous compatriots, both of whom exploit their helplessness in a variety of ways.

The underclass of illegal aliens tends to be vulnerable to serious criminal activity like drug-smuggling. Though the overwhelming majority of immigrants coming into the United States illegally are upright persons, who probably obey the law at home, some are tempted to break U.S. laws when narcotics smugglers offer them money to carry cocaine or heroin across the border.

The growth of an underclass composed predominantly of Mexican illegals is of increasing concern to U.S. officials, particularly those in charge of law enforcement along the border. Alan E. Eliason was chief of the Border Patrol's San Diego Sector, the largest of nine Border Patrol sectors and the No. 1 port of entry for immigrants from Mexico, when I interviewed him in March 1986. The sector covers an area of 5,000 square miles, much of it scarred by mountains and canyons which make ideal hiding places for anyone evading the law. That year, apprehensions of illegal immigrants would spurt up to the record level of nearly 1.8 million. Chief Eliason was understandably concerned. What bothered him most was that "a process is going on completely outside the norm of this society." He explained:

> We see building up in the United States a population who live outside that norm, outside the law. Most of them are exploited, much as the slaves were. They are a subclass which is not participating in the democratic process. What attachment do they have to this country?[16]

Eliason expressed pride in America's tradition as the haven of persecuted people everywhere. "I am the grandson of immigrants," he pointed out. He favored bringing into the country as many immigrants as it can absorb, but by legal means, under a set quota.

***

What is wrong with allowing people from other nations to migrate to the United States? Wasn't this country founded, after all, on the principle that others have a right to enjoy its fruits as long as they work hard and obey the law? The history of the United States is, essentially, the history of successive waves of immigrants landing on its shores and contributing everything they could to its growth into a great nation. As the inscription on the Statue of Liberty proclaims:

> *Give me your tired, your poor,*
> *Your huddled masses yearning to breathe free,*
> *The wretched refuse of your teeming shore.*
> *Send these, the homeless, tempest-tossed to me,*
> *I lift my lamp beside the open door!*

Immigrants have traditionally been accepted in America. Sooner or later, they have become assimilated into the mainstream and evolved into citizens every bit as hard-working, law-abiding and loyal as earlier settlers. Exactly the same pattern has characterized Mexican immigrants: They, too, have taken their place in American society along with the rest of us as people who work hard and assume their share of responsibility for maintaining a stable and prosperous country. The problem, however, is not those who come here legally, in conformity with the nation's immigration laws; or who, like the ones who fled the ravages of the Mexican Revolution lasting from 1910 until the late 1920s, have received special dispensation to remain. We must and should continue to extend, as always, a cordial welcome to such persons, among them the one million Mexicans who are projected to enter the United States legally in the 1990s. Rather, it is those who enter the country illegally, in violation of its laws, who are the problem. It is about them we must be rightfully concerned.

The issue is clear: Immigration that is legal, hence under the control of the appropriate authorities of the host nation — in this case, the United States — is welcome. Immigration that is illegal, hence uncontrolled, can by its very nature become a menace to American institutions and must therefore be brought under control before it is too late.

This study documents how our institutions are under threat from rising illegal immigration and proposes some possible solutions to the problem. The threat to our national sovereignty is, of course, primordial. That is implicit in the challenge to our system of law—and respect for the law—which is violated by the very act of crossing into U.S. territory without the proper immigration papers; without, that is, the permission of our duly constituted authorities.

The reasons for such concern are many and will be examined in detail in the course of this work. In doing so, every effort will be made to understand the root causes of the illegal migration into this country—chiefly two: abysmal economic conditions and high rates of population growth in Mexico — and to sympathize with the victims thereof. In that connection, stress will be laid upon the important, perhaps decisive role that the Mexican Government can play in completing reforms that should ultimately benefit the mass of Mexicans and induce them to stay home.

Meanwhile, if existing realities appear harsh and sometimes seem to cast Mexico in a negative light, that is by no means the author's design. Unfortunately, they are the product of a history that has too often militated against the well-being of the Mexican people. Perhaps we can begin to understand the phenomenon of illegal immigration by first putting it in some historical context.

2

The Origins of Mexican Immigration

MEXICAN IMMIGRATION into the United States is a phenomenon that is both quite old and relatively new. In the years following Mexico's independence, in 1821, few Mexicans cared to venture much beyond the central highlands where the bulk of the population, numbering about 6.5 million, lived. For three decades after Mexico ceded to the United States the vast lands that comprise the present states of Arizona, California, New Mexico, Nevada, Utah, and part of Colorado, Mexican immigration was but a trickle. Those lands were of course already occupied mainly by people of Mexican origin, who themselves had once been immigrants in the wake of the Spanish *conquistadores*. It was not until the early part of the 20th century that Mexicans began to migrate north of the border in large numbers.

The reverse had been the trend a century before: increasing numbers of Americans migrated from the United States southward into Mexico. After the American Revolution, a steady stream of colonists from the newly independent Union flowed into Texas, which then belonged to Mexico. As early as 1785, Philip Nolan arrived there to engage in horse-trading, and a dozen years later Secretary of State Thomas Jefferson was curious enough to write him seeking information about Texas. Nolan was among the first of a long line of adventurers, including would-be empire builders like Aaron Burr, who were increasingly attracted to Texas. Between 1806 and 1819, the area between the Arroyo Hondo and Sabine River was a no-man's-land infested chiefly by outlaws from the United States.

The first organized, legitimate effort to settle Texas was made in 1821 by Moses Austin, who had been involved in a variety of mining and land deals in Missouri and Arkansas. A man of vision, Austin obtained from the short-lived Mexican emperor, Agustín Iturbide, a concession to establish a Roman Catholic colony in Texas. But before he could launch the project, he died, leaving his son Stephen to carry on. When Stephen Austin arrived in Texas, in the summer of 1821, it contained only two inhabited towns, San Antonio and Goliad (then known, respectively, as Béjar and La Bahía), with a combined population of 2,516. After four months exploring what he called "a howling wilderness,"[1] the younger Austin went to Mexico City and got Iturbide to confirm his father's concession. It was agreed that Texas should be colonized by Americans, and that Austin would bring in several hundred of them by offering generous parcels of land and a seven-year tax exemption to encourage them to develop it.

By 1825, Americans were flooding into Texas. Alarmed, Mexico a year later tried to restrict the immigration by imposing such conditions as adherence to the Catholic faith—conditions the settlers, now numbering an impressive 12,000, ignored. Their stubborn attitude soon became the object of serious dispute. By 1832, they were demanding a separate state within the Mexican republic, which was supported by the legislature of what was then the state of Coahuila y Texas but rejected by Mexico City. In an attempt to force the Texans to yield, the ruler of Mexico, General Antonio López de Santa Anna, sent 4,000 troops against them.

Led by Austin, the Texas colonists banded themselves together under the banner of "Texas First"—within the Mexican Republic if possible, outside it if necessary. In December 1835, they overwhelmed Santa Anna's forces at Béjar—better known as San Antonio—and took their commanding general prisoner. On March 2, 1836, as Santa Anna prepared to sound the *degüello* and bathe the Alamo in blood, the Republic of Texas was born and a decade of internecine strife set in.

President Andrew Jackson quickly recognized the Texas republic, and was prevented from seeking its annexation only by the opposition of the North, which objected to Texas because it favored slavery. By 1845, however, the expansionist forces led by James K. Polk had grown strong enough to elect him President and annex the new republic. That alarmed the Mexicans: Polk's eagerness to acquire also California, Arizona, and New Mexico was well-known for he had offered to buy them.

Perhaps the most significant period in the early relations between the United States and Mexico after both attained independence was between 1836 and 1847, when a state of almost perpetual warfare prevailed between them. Basically, it was a war of nationalisms,[2] with newly independent Mexico attempting to define itself as a nation-state while the United States eagerly sought to expand its territory in pursuit of "manifest destiny." It determined forever their size and geography. Mexico lost the war, and with it more than half its territory and immense natural resources; these losses had a traumatic effect upon the Mexicans from which they— the elite, at least — have yet to fully recover. The United States was correspondingly augmented in size, reaching now from the Atlantic to the Pacific and from the Great Lakes to the Río Grande—known in Mexico as the Río Bravo—and acquiring fabulous resources such as the rich oilfields and ranchlands of Texas. Those acquisitions provided the basis, in fact, for the rise of the United States as a world power.

The issue that precipitated the 1836-47 war was Texas. That "half-nation,"[3] as Parkes so aptly called it, had from the earliest days exercised a decisive influence upon the countries lying on either side of it. The huge territory first attracted white colonists as far back as 1682, when the great French explorer, Sieur de La Salle, reached the mouth of the Mississippi and founded Louisiana. But it was not until the beginning of the 18th century, when the Spaniards set up a system of missions, that colonies began to take root; one of the most famous of those missions was the Alamo, in San Antonio, which was to become a searing symbol of Texan nationalism.

Mexico was unable to maintain a stable government throughout the 1836-47 decade, during which no fewer than six different constitutions were decreed by as many regimes. Unable to govern in the center, its leaders were scarcely able to exercise their authority in the outlying north where a U.S. Presidential emissary sought to negotiate with them a boundary line between Mexico and Texas. When his envoy was expelled from Mexico, Polk ordered General Zachary Taylor to march to the Río Grande and maintain a line there. On April 25, 1846, the Mexican cavalry engaged Taylor's forces and

Polk promptly requested Congress to declare war on its southern neighbor.

The landing of General Winfield Scott in Veracruz signalled the beginning of the end, for he soon decimated Santa Anna's army and pushed on to Mexico City itself. The Mexicans, even under Santa Anna, fought valiantly for three weeks but superior American arms and generalship inevitably won the day. Mexican courage was symbolized by the cadets who fought Scott at Chapultepec and who ever since have been enshrined in Mexican hearts as the *"niños heroes"* — boy heroes. On September 14, 1847, which would go down as one of its darkest days, Mexico formally surrendered the capital to Scott.

Under the Treaty of Guadalupe Hidalgo signed on February 2, 1848, Mexico agreed to recognize the annexation of Texas, which covered 384,958 square miles, and ceded to the United States an area of 530,706 square miles. *All* of its territory would probably have been forfeited had Polk, who for a change exercised restraint, heeded the clamor of the extremists in his manifest destiny party; instead, he agreed to the treaty as Scott and his personal emissary, Nicholas P. Trist, had drafted it.

Mexico had left behind in the conquered territories many thousands of people, including both Indians and Mexican settlers. An estimated 75,000 Mexicans chose to become U.S. citizens,[4] an option provided in the Guadalupe Hidalgo Treaty, and remained permanently. Their presence north of the Río Grande, which finally became the borderline between Mexico and the United States, had the effect of rendering the new "border" basically unreal: As they always had, people on both sides traveled back and forth, exchanged goods and services, intermarried, shared the same religious, cultural and linguistic traditions, in utter freedom. Even after formal customs houses and immigration checkpoints were established, nothing really interfered with the human intercourse that had been going on for centuries. In time, the border seemed to behave like a "third nation," its inhabitants equally remote in many ways from their respective central governments.

In retrospect, it was back then that the United States "lost" control over the border with Mexico. Better said, it never enjoyed totally effective control. The border had always been and perhaps will always remain, porous. To that extent, it was probably unlike most borders between nations elsewhere in the world, and in some respects is perhaps unique. It is within that context that we must, if we wish to be realistic, view the problem of Mexicans who enter the United States illegally.

If few Mexicans ventured northward into the new American states in the decades following the 1848 war, it was largely because they were neither readily accessible nor attractive. Those with a taste for adventure were discouraged by the arid and empty vastness that lay to the north, and by the absence of good roads or rail lines. Nor were there many good jobs in the underpopulated Southwest to draw them there. Meanwhile, Anglos flooded into California with the Gold Rush that began in 1848, and two years later it became a state. In time, Mexicans became a minority there and everywhere else in the Southwest.

In those days, there was no real distinction between "legal" and "illegal" immigration. To most people, there was little to distinguish one side of the border from the other. They crossed back and forth at will, since no sharp line existed between the two countries either geographically or culturally: With the exception of Texas, which was mostly Anglo, the inhabitants of the ceded territories were largely of Mexican origin, spoke the same language and practised the same religion as their Mexican neighbors. In any case, the Southwestern states or territories themselves, not Washington, controlled the flow of immigrants, and seemed not averse to Mexicans coming in. It was not until 1875 that the first Federal regulatory legislation—which barred convicts and prostitutes—was enacted.[5]

Today's prevalent mode of illegal immigration from Mexico, "entry without inspection," or slipping across unguarded portions of the border, would have been technically impossible before the last decade of the century since there were no inspection stations to pass through. The Federal Bureau of Immigration, then part of the Treasury Department, did not establish the first inspection stations at ports of entry on the Mexican and Canadian borders until 1891.

The first surge of Mexican workers into the United States from their central highlands began in the 1880s, when a railroad was laid linking Mexico with the United States, mainly the Southwest.[6] That also helped populate Mexico's own northern states. Largely built by American and European investors with the encouragement of the Mexican dictator, General Porfirio Díaz, the new railway ended the isolation of the bulk of Mexico's population and for the first time permitted it mobility. Workers who were recruited to build or repair tracks in Mexico followed the rail route into the United States, where they were hired for similar work. (Ironically, Díaz's new railroad contributed to the dictatorship's demise: the revolutionary chiefs who overthrew him would commandeer passenger and freight cars to rush troops against his military successors.)

Now mobile, Mexican workers found themselves regularly welcomed by ranchers and other employers in the Southwest during the last two decades of the 19th century. Normal sources of docile foreign labor had dried up with the passage of immigration laws, in 1882 and 1885, to exclude Chinese and bar the importation of foreign "contract laborers"; Mexican workers filled the gap.

Another factor that made hiring Mexican workers attractive was that most of them returned home when no longer needed. The come-and-go migration of Mexican workers grew in the late 1800s, while those who settled permanently in the United States were relatively modest in number. Only 100,000 persons of Mexican birth were recorded in the U.S. census of 1900. Few citizens of our southern neighbor cared then to move north—a somewhat odd phenomenon which would reverse itself in little more than a decade.

These early Mexican farm migrants were "pushed" out of their country, to a great extent, by Díaz's policy of concentrating ownership of the land in the hands of a relatively tiny group of friends and collaborators, who simply dispossessed small farmers and created vast *haciendas* farmed by *peones*, virtual serfs. Other "push" factors under Díaz were rampant inflation and poverty, to which was added severe repression.

3

Mexico's Explosive Population Growth — Source of Illegal Migration

AS IMMIGRATION from Mexico mounted at the turn of the century, so did Washington's concern over illegal entry into the country. A report of the Commissioner General of Immigration, in 1903, spoke of increasing difficulties involving illegal Mexican border crossings. Washington was equally concerned about the persistent smuggling of Chinese aliens through Mexico.

Indeed, U.S. immigration officials were at first more concerned over the illegal entry of Chinese nationals than of any other foreign group, including Mexicans. Many of the Chinese set sail from Cuba, which at one point harbored approximately 30,000 persons of Chinese birth. The earliest restrictive legislation singling out a given nationality for exclusion, passed in 1882, was in fact directed at the Chinese. At that time, Chinese labor "was flooding and depressing the labor market" in the United States, according to a study made by Donald R. Coppock, then Deputy Associate Commissioner, Domestic Control, of the INS. The restrictive legislation proved counterproductive, however, and "increasingly large numbers of Orientals and other inadmissible aliens resorted to illegal entry," reported Coppock.[1]

In 1904, as a result, the Commissioner General of Immigration assigned a small group of mounted inspectors to patrol the entire border on horseback—forerunners of today's Border Patrol. Never totalling more than 76, it was basically a token force that proved "woefully inadequate" to grapple with the illegals problem. The Commissioner General reported that illegal entries across the U.S.-

19

Mexican border were "constantly on the increase."[2] For every 100 aliens apprehended, 1,000 eluded detection, Coppock found.

Two upheavals early in this century swelled migration from Mexico to record heights.

One was the Mexican Revolution commencing in 1910 and lasting nearly two decades, which drove hundreds of thousands north in search not only of work but, more important yet, of personal security. Of a total population of 15 million, an estimated 10 percent emigrated to the United States between 1910 and 1930, according to most authorities. One analyst, Luis Horacio Durán writes:

> A minor 'mass' migration occurred [from 1910 to 1918] because of the 'push' factor that represented the threat of the Mexican Revolution to some of the inhabitants in the northern states of Sonora, Chihuahua, Coahuila, and Nuevo León.[3]

The National Council of La Raza estimates that "about 685,000 legal immigrants" were included in the total driven north by revolution. Among them were many professionals and members of the middle class. In a monograph on Hispanics and immigration, NCLR reports:

> The immigrants of 1910-1930 were more diverse in their socio-economic status than later Mexican immigrants; they included many political activists, professionals, and business owners as well as individuals with limited education and training.[4]

The other upheaval which drove Mexicans northward was the outbreak of World War I in 1914 which, concurrent with the Revolution during the next four years, boosted the demand of U.S. farms, factories, mines and railroads for unskilled labor. From 1910 to 1920, an estimated 500,000 Mexicans settled in the United States.[5]

By 1930, reports the Bureau of the Census, 640,000 persons of Mexican birth resided in this country—which is close to the number of *legal* immigrants reported by NCLR. That represented a better than sixfold increase since 1900. The Department of Labor put the total at more than one million.[6]

Illegal immigration from Mexico rose concurrently. It continued steadily upward during the 1920s, as U.S. immigration policies increasingly restricted legal entry. Otherwise ineligible Mexican citizens and third-country nationals slipped into the United States across the southern border almost with impunity. To staunch the flow, the U.S. Border Patrol came into being on May 28, 1924, but its efforts were hampered from the start by a sorry lack of personnel: it had only 450 officers to police the length and breadth of both the Canadian and Mexican borders, a total of 7,525 miles.[7]

The fact is that the smuggling of aliens from Cuba to Florida and the Gulf Coast areas continued on a large scale even after the Border Patrol was founded. To combat the problem, Congress passed an act on February 27, 1925, which provided funds for a "coast and land border patrol" and also, for the first time, authorized certain officers of the Bureau of Immigration to issue warrants under the laws regulating aliens, and to arrest any alien who attempted to enter the United States in violation of such laws.

The Immigration and Nationality Act of June 27, 1952 — better known as the McCarran-Walter Act — substantially incorporated most of the legislation on immigration passed since 1925, and added one significant proviso: Border Patrol and other law enforcement officers were permitted to board and search a conveyance suspected of harboring or transporting aliens, anywhere in the United States. The primary authority under which the Border Patrol operates today is contained in Section 103 of the Act, which states in part:

> [The Attorney General of the United States shall] have the power and duty to control and guard the boundaries and borders of the United States against the illegal entry of aliens and shall, in his discretion, appoint for that purpose such number of employees of the service as to him shall appear necessary and proper.[8]

This authority has been delegated, in practice, to the Commissioner of Immigration and Naturalization.

A substantial return migration of Mexicans to their own country occurred during the Great Depression of the 1930s, but with the economic boom that accompanied World War II the flow northward jumped again. In 1942, with the United States experiencing an acute shortage of labor due to the military draft of millions of citizens in their most productive years, Washington and Mexico City signed their first migrant labor agreement. Popularly known as the *bracero* program — from *brazo*, arm — it permitted the legal importation of Mexican workers for U.S. farms on a seasonal basis, under Section 3 of the Immigration Act of February 5, 1917.

A continued shortage of domestic labor in the United States after the war resulted in the enactment of Public Law 78, which provided for the importation of agricultural laborers. In the peak year of 1959, a total of 500,000 Mexican workers were admitted into the United States legally. But Public Law 78 was terminated on December 31, 1964, at Washington's insistence, and the legal importation of Mexican agricultural workers fell drastically.

The bracero program turned out to be a powerful stimulus to illegal immigration. The number of legal contracts offered under the program consistently fell far below the number of Mexican workers wanting to work. As a result, many arrived without contracts, undercutting the labor standards of legally contracted workers in the process.

Contacts and networks created by workers coming in as braceros were used to aid the subsequent illegal immigration of friends and relatives. A Presidential Commission on Migratory Labor warned in 1951:

> The number of deportations and voluntary departures has continuously mounted each year . . . . In its newly achieved proportions, [the wetback traffic] is virtually an invasion.[9]

In 1954, the Eisenhower Administration responded to the alarm in the Southwest over the swelling tide of illegal settlers with "Operation Wetback," a massive Immigration and Naturalization Service roundup that ultimately expelled more than one million Mexican aliens. (The term "wetback" derived from the fact that many, but by no means all, illegal migrants forded the Río Grande to the U.S. side on the backs of others because they could not swim.) The sweeping expulsions deterred illegal immigration for several years. Triumphantly, but with little prophetic insight, the Department of Justice declared in 1955:

The so-called 'wetback' problem no longer exists. The decline in the number of 'wetbacks' found in the United States, even after concentrated and vigorous enforcement efforts were pursued through the year, reveals that this is no longer, as in the past, a problem of border control. The border has been secured.[10]

But illegal immigration from Mexico surged again after Congress ended the legal authority for the bracero program in 1964. Tens of thousands of Mexican workers poured into the United States illegally, in search of jobs on American farms and, increasingly, in urban factories and service industries. INS apprehensions of illegals rose from 110,000 in 1965 to half a million in 1972, and in 1977 broke the one-million mark for the first time since Operation Wetback. Repeal of the bracero program had simply driven it "underground." As Coppock reported:

Statistics concerning the relationship between the importation of Mexican laborers and deportable aliens located reveal that as the number of contracted Mexican laborers declined, the number of deportable aliens apprehended increased.[11]

There was a steady rise in the number of apprehensions from 1965 to 1979, followed by a drop during the next three years. Beginning in 1983, the number of apprehensions increased again, only this time more sharply than in the period up to 1979. They persistently remained above the one-million mark, reaching an all-time high of 1.77 million in 1986. Another period of declining apprehensions started in 1987, after passage of the Immigration Reform and Control Act (IRCA) in 1986, and by 1988 they had dropped below one million for the first time since the beginning of the decade. Then the trend toward increasing apprehensions resumed in the following year, and reached nearly 1.17 million in 1990. (See Table 1.)

The coincidence between the steadily rising number of apprehensions of illegals and the collapse of the Mexican economy, toward the end of 1982, is striking. It lays bare the co-relationship between deteriorating economic opportunities in Mexico and the number of Mexicans who, though lacking proper immigration documents, are impelled northward. Clearly, what happened was that the economy,

TABLE 1
Apprehensions of Illegal Aliens 1965-1990

1965	110,371	1979	1,069,400
1966	138,520	1980	910,361
1967	161,608	1981	975,780
1968	212,057	1982	970,246
1969	283,557	1983	1,251,351
1970	345,353	1984	1,246,981
1972	505,949	1985	1,348,749
1973	655,968	1986	1,767,400
1974	788,145	1987	1,190,488
1975	756,819	1988	954,243
1976	866,433	1989	1,008,148
1977	1,033,427	1990	1,169,939
1978	1,047,687		

Source: Immigration and Naturalization Service

which buckled under the weight of excessive debt, government mismanagement, corruption, and plummeting oil prices was responsible for the worsening of the country's already mediocre job-creation record. Illegal entries spiraled. Immigration expert Michael Teitelbaum has commented on this phenomenon:

> The economic crisis that began in Mexico in 1982 led to a massive flight of capital, a near-default on Mexico's foreign debt, and a 90-percent devaluation of the peso. The result was flat or negative economic growth, rising unemployment, large declines in real wages, and growing wage differentials between Mexico and the United States. The effects on Mexican migration to the United States were predictable: apparent increases in illegal flows, as evidenced by sharply higher numbers of arrests without commensurate expansion of the enforcement effort.[12]

With the economy stagnant for most of the decade, nearly half of Mexico's labor force of 30 million workers was unemployed or underemployed in 1990. Approximately 13-15 million under-utilized workers form a pool of candidates for illegal migration to the

United States—a pool that grows by some 400,000 to 500,000 potential migrants a year. The workers who manage to enter the United States legally now tend to be overwhelmingly young and poorly educated. A study done by North and Houston in 1976 showed that 78 percent were between the ages of 16 and 34, with an average of only 4.9 years of formal schooling (compared to 12.6 years for the U.S. labor force).[13]

Mexico's dominance as a source of illegal immigration was apparent in the statistics gathered by the INS on aliens legalized under IRCA. Its Legalization Application Statistics issued in mid-1990 showed that nearly 75 percent of all legalized aliens were Mexican, 70 percent were between the ages of 15 and 34, and 67 percent were males. "Entry without inspection," or slipping across the border, was the way 92 percent of all legalized Mexican aliens entered the United States. For non-Mexican illegal aliens, the predominant mode was to enter with a legitimate tourist visa and then overstay, accord-ing to the INS report.[14]

Explosive population growth was the force behind the quantum leap of illegal Mexican immigration in the 1950s, and sustains it now. At the end of its revolution in the late 1920s, Mexico was demographically stagnant as well as physically, economically and politically prostrate. Its pre-1910 population had declined sharply during a decade of upheaval characterized by civil war, political chaos, economic crisis and out-migration, falling from 15.1 million in 1910 to 14.3 million in 1921, according to Francisco Alba's research.[15]

As Mexico recovered from the ravages of revolution in the 1930s, public health, education, and nutrition improved markedly. Historically high mortality rates, particularly among infants, plummeted. On the eve of the 1910 revolt, a working-class or peasant mother of six children faced the probability that two of them would die in infancy. Mexico's fertility rate was high, but high mortality was the governor on the nation's demographic engine. By 1970, infant mortality, thanks to great strides in public health and education, had been reduced fivefold. A mother of six had a much better than even chance that all of her children would reach adulthood. Because of what some demographers have called the "Death Dearth,"

1 in 3 children die.

Mexico's population tripled between 1930 and 1970—from 17 million to 52 million—and grew markedly younger in the process, note Bouvier and Simcox.[16]

The result of the lower mortality and continued high birth rates was a massive increase in the working age population in the 1950s. Mexico's labor force grew from less than 5 million in 1930 to 14.6 million in 1970, by which time the number of new job-seekers was approaching nearly 800,000 a year. Migration from farm to city put additional pressure on Mexico's labor market. About two-thirds of the population resided and worked in rural Mexico in 1930; by 1970, 60 percent of its people and 56 percent of its labor force lived in urban centers. Over the next two decades, Mexico became a fully urbanized nation, with 73 percent of its population living in cities and towns, according to the United Nations.[17]

Rapid population growth and mass flight to the cities seriously outdistanced Mexico's job-creating ability. During the 1980s, the number of job-seekers entering the market each year grew to 900,000, and will exceed a million annually in the 1990s.[18] Changes in the Mexican economy intensified the challenge of absorbing such a vast amount of new workers. While the industrial sector was ringing up impressive growth statistics through much of the 1960s and 1970s— 6 percent or more a year—agriculture was beginning a long slide downhill, and that drove huge numbers of small farmers and campesinos into the cities or to the United States in search of work. In fact, there is a direct co-relation between the crisis in Mexican agriculture, which has been chronic for almost two decades — thus antedating the general economic crisis of the 1980s—and the pronounced trend toward illegal entry into the United States after 1968.

Mexico's labor force in the 1970s was growing at an unprecedented 4.4 percent annually, but millions were limited in their usefulness to its changing economy due to poor education and training. For most of its statistically impressive growth, the country's industrial sector relied increasingly on capital-intensive processes: jobs added did not match production growth. Job creation in the 1970s approached only 400,000 a year, just half the total needed. Mexico's protectionist policies, its isolation from the international economy, its emphasis on costly public sector prestige projects, its neglect of rural development, and its intrusive, over-regulating bureaucracy had combined to stifle job creation.

As the last decade of the century commenced, prospects for creating enough new jobs for Mexico's youth did not appear promising. The economic reforms initiated by President Salinas, though encouraging, did not seem likely to absorb one million new job-seekers each year for two reasons. The first was that the reforms had not gone far enough: Above all, the Government was unable to resolve the agricultural crisis and in fact it continued to worsen, thus practically assuring continuation of the peasant exodus into Mexican cities and the United States indefinitely. The second was the growing application of high technology, partly due to Mexico's entry into the General Tariffs and Trade Agreement, which is bound to leap forward with the signing of a free trade agreement with the United States and Canada. This will eventually eliminate altogether or curtail drastically the operations of many industries that have traditionally absorbed manual labor. In the event, very large numbers of urban workers are likely to join the peasant armies heading for El Norte throughout the decade and beyond.

4

Illegal Migration Violates U.S. Sovereignty

BY DEFINITION, the movement of persons or goods from one nation-state to another nation-state employing illicit means— without, that is, obtaining explicit written permission from the authorities of the second state—is a violation of that state's sovereignty. Webster's Dictionary defines sovereignty as "supreme power over a body politic" and as "freedom from external control." It is an internationally accepted principle that all the 159 independent countries which belong to the United Nations have the right, if not the duty, to guard and protect their borders, and enjoy full sovereign powers to determine what persons or goods shall be allowed to enter and leave the territory of a given nation-state. This is the right of all nations under international law and is jealously guarded by them.

Although the U.S. Constitution does not expressly state that Congress "shall control the borders" of the United States, regulating entry into a nation's territory is a right incident to the sovereignty of the nation. This right is fundamental to what is defined as sovereign, and the U.S. Supreme Court has never questioned it. It is a centuries-old concept inherited from our European common law jurisprudential framework. As Emmerich de Vattel stated in his benchmark work, *The Law of Nations:*

> Every nation has the right to refuse to admit a foreigner into the country . . . . What it owes to itself, the care for its own safety, gives it this right; and, in virtue of its natural liberty, it belongs to the nation to judge whether its circumstances will or will not justify the admission of the foreigner.[1]

28

Nations are thus within their sovereign rights to determine which foreigners may enter their countries, whether to travel, work, study, do business, obtain permanent residence, or for any other purpose. They are also within their sovereign rights to control, through the issuance of visas, work permits, and other documentation, who is allowed to cross the boundaries of that state and to be admitted as immigrants for permanent residence.

The question of who may immigrate into a country is held under international law to be the exclusive, sovereign, unilateral right of the recipient nation to determine. However, Mexican critics, including officials, who have accused the United States of taking unilateral decisions with respect to immigration ignore, or overlook, this sovereign right when it comes to illegal immigration into the United States. Yet such critics are often the first to uphold Mexico's sovereignty in immigration matters, and support unquestioningly — as they should — their own government's unilateral right to pick and choose who can enter their country.

The Mexican Government rejects out of hand any claim by foreign persons to the right to enter its territory illegally, without a proper visa or other prescribed documentation. In the justifiable exercise of its own sovereign rights, Mexico long ago made the decision not to allow immigrants into the country to take up permanent residence except in a very limited number of cases; mainly, these involved small special categories of which Mexico considered itself in need, a policy it still upholds rigorously. Its *Ley General de Población* — General Population Law — the basic law which, *inter alia*, governs immigration and the residency status and requirements of foreigners in Mexico, requires all immigrants to obtain, in advance, a special Mexican Government immigration permit. Such a permit

> [will] be granted primarily to scientists and technicians . . .
> in disciplines insufficiently filled by Mexicans, as well as to
> [foreign] investors. . . .[2]

More than six decades of illegal crossings of our southern border have to some extent created in many Mexican minds a sense that the illegals are "entitled" to act as they do. (This is at times reinforced by U.S. Government acquiescence in such crossings, but more often by ineffectual measures to prevent them.) A more extreme view is that the border is not legitimate, has no validity. Some of the more radical Chicano groups in the United States even defend illegal immigration as not really illegal: Believing the U.S. acquisition of the Southwest by military conquest and the subsequent Treaty of Guadalupe Hidalgo to be illegitimate, they hold that the border so created lacks legitimacy.

In some areas, the border has in fact become a virtual "no-man's-land." Such is the case of the San Diego Sector, where the movement of illegal immigrants is much greater than at any other U.S. entry point. The Soccer Field/Zapata Canyon staging area mentioned earlier, where hundreds of Mexicans congregate every evening before attempting nighttime crossings into San Diego County surreptitiously, is of course U.S. territory. Nothing better illustrates the mockery made of the sovereignty of the United States and of its right to control its border, than the illegals' utilization of U.S. territory to engage in their illicit enterprise on a continuous basis. Neither Mexico, nor any other sovereign nation, would countenance such flagrant abuse of its homeland for a single instant.

***

The rapid expansion of illegal immigration into the United States is a threat to the integrity of its legal system in general. By its very nature, illegal immigration constitutes a violation of U.S. immigration legislation, and contributes to a growing sub-culture of lawlessness in which a host of federal, state, and local laws and ordinances are regularly violated.

The U.S. Immigration and Nationality Act, as amended, establishes a system for the issuance of immigration visas to persons who wish to enter the United States. It is an elaborate system of preferences, carefully worked out by Congress over the years, based on family relationships with U.S. citizens and legal permanent resident aliens in the United States; in some instances, it is based upon possession of various skills which are in short supply and are needed in the United States. In addition, the INA provides for maximum numerical limitations on non-immediate family immigrants from any one country, including Mexico—a limitation which amounts to a maximum of about 25,000 visas per country per year.[3]

Our visa-screening procedures (both for immigrant and non-immigrant visas), performed by our consuls at embassies and consulates overseas, are mandated by legislation enacted by Congress. Visa screening serves the public interest in keeping out certain classes of persons deemed by Congress as undesirable for admission to the United States on grounds of security, public health, criminal background, or general public interest. Some categories of persons barred from entry into the United States with immigrant visas can be admitted for short temporary periods with nonimmigrant visas, provided that waivers are obtained in advance. It should also be noted that some of the grounds for exclusion, most notably those involving security, are significantly modified, and in a few instances eliminated, under the Immigration and Nationality Act of 1990. Section 212 of the INA, as amended, currently specifies 33 categories of aliens who are ineligible to receive visas and who are thus excluded from admission to the United States. (See Appendix A for a complete list of these categories.)

Most of the 33 categories of aliens excluded under the INA did not come into being until after 1891, a time when we began to seriously consider, and to legislate, the exclusion of many of the undesirable categories specified in the Act. The legislative philosophy of immigration adopted at that time was perhaps best expressed by Senator Henry Cabot Lodge, Sr., who in 1896 observed that:

> In careless strength, with generous hand, we have kept our gates wide open to all the world. If we do not close them, we should at least place sentinels beside them to challenge those that would pass through. The gates which admit men to the United States and to citizenship in the great Republic should no longer be left unguarded.[4]

Illegal immigration into the United States violates the INA and its carefully mandated mechanisms of visa screening. Clearly, illegal immigrants who have entered by crossing U.S. borders surreptitiously have deliberately violated our immigration laws. Section 8 USC 1325 makes "entry without inspection," or entry by false and misleading representations, a misdemeanor subject to jail terms of six months and fines. Subsequent convictions are felonies subject to jail terms of two years. Similarly, a person who obtained a tourist visa to enter the United States but did so with the secret intention of engaging in remunerative employment (which is prohibited to holders of tourist visas), and who overstayed beyond the six months normally allowed as the maximum amount of time in the United States under a tourist visa, has likewise deliberately flouted our immigration laws.

In practically every case, adult illegal immigrants are conscious of the fact that they have knowingly violated U.S. law, but do so because they know that they would be ineligible for a normal immigrant visa, or because they do not wish to go through the lengthy wait that an immigrant visa would entail. (For Mexicans, it may take up to nine, and as many as a dozen years for some family preference categories.) The ease with which illegal immigrants are able to enter the United States by simply walking undetected across the border mocks our immigrant visa issuance system.*

The illegals traffic, among its other evils, does an injustice to the more than two million persons on our immigrant visa waiting lists at U.S. embassies overseas, including the more than 20 percent who are Mexicans. Silvestre Reyes, the Chief U.S. Border Patrol Agent in McAllen, Texas, put it succinctly in a newspaper interview in which he said, "the country that fails to control its borders will fail to control its history."[5]

By far the greatest volume of illegal immigration moves across the Mexico-U.S. border and involves Mexican nationals. (Central Americans are a distant second.) Mexican (and Central American) border violators enjoy a distinct advantage over persons in Asia, Europe, and Africa who wish to immigrate to the United States but do not share a land border with it that makes stealing across easy. Normally, they must apply for an immigrant visa, get a petition filed in their behalf, then wait years before the possibility of immigrating to the U.S. arises. It is a classic example of a cheat being rewarded while the person who acts lawfully—i.e., applies for an immigrant visa at a U.S. immigration facility—is penalized.

---

*As a test, I have walked across the border at various points that were not legal ports of entry, without detection. In one instance, I came to a door-size opening which I was able to straddle without discomfort — one leg on the Mexican side, the other on the American — and, again, without being detected. There was no law enforcement officer within miles.

To add to the irony, Mexicans who choose to enter the United States illicitly violate automatically their own country's immigration law as well as ours. Under Mexican law, it is unlawful to travel abroad without appropriate documents, including a valid Mexican passport— which, of course, the vast majority of Mexican illegal aliens do not possess. (It is also a violation of Mexican law to leave the country other than by a legally designated point of exit, under the 1979 General Population Law.) The same is true of illegal immigrants from such Central American countries as El Salvador, Guatemala, and Nicaragua. In fact, most of the illegal immigrants from those countries appear to be unskilled persons with a limited education (usually no higher than fifth grade level) and would be unlikely to even try to obtain passports or other appropriate documentation from their home governments as it would require too much money, time, and trouble.

***

The violation of U.S. immigration law inherent in crossing the border surreptitiously is not the only threat that illegal immigration poses to the American legal system. Indeed, illegal immigration invites, and appears to foster, violations of U.S. legislation in a multitude of fields. Living a life beyond the law logically encourages a culture of lawlessness.

Typically, since the illegal immigrant has violated U.S. immigration law to get here, he wants to maintain a very low profile and keep his identity and status concealed from the authorities. In many jobs, however, the law requires that he have a Social Security number in order to work in the United States. Usually, the illegal immigrant will therefore either use someone else's valid Social Security number or obtain a false one. In so doing, he commits fraud and at the same time violates the Social Security law. The illegal alien's use of a false Social Security card in a range of official and unofficial transactions compounds the original violation. Besides, such practices, multiplied on an astronomical scale given the volume of illegal immigrants using fake Social Security documents, tend to confuse the records of the Social Security Administration. Those records are relied upon for accuracy by millions of American citizens and permanent resident aliens, who will someday expect to receive Social Security pensions.

Because it is imperative for them to remain inconspicuous and out of sight of the authorities, illegal aliens often end up violating various other laws. Many of them insist, for example, on being paid in cash in order to avoid having to pay U.S. income taxes or file U.S. income tax returns—a practice which unscrupulous American employers may be only too willing to countenance. Illegals are prone, also, to commit fraud in order to acquire a driver's license. It is not unusual for them to obtain fraudulent birth certificates to enable them to qualify for amnesty, which was granted to certain classes of illegals by the 1986 Immigration Reform Control Act, or to establish a bogus identity so that they may even claim U.S. citizenship. (See Appendix B for a list of the principal violations of the law involving offenses connected with illegal immigration into the United States.)

Illegal male immigrants between 18 and 25 are also apt to violate the U.S. Selective Service law by not registering.[6] In many instances, illegal aliens violate housing codes by, for example, crowding more immigrants into apartments or houses in immigrant neighborhoods than local codes allow. Illegal aliens, by virtue of their status and avoidance of contact with the authorities, also present a standing invitation to their employers (whether U.S. citizens, permanent resident aliens, or illegal immigrants themselves) to violate U.S. health and safety, wage and hour, and labor laws.

Violations of features of our immigration laws denying admission to the United States to paupers and to persons "likely to become a public charge" have a long history dating back to the early years of the Republic. Thus in 1837 Justice Thompson, in the *City of New York v. Miln,* gave this view of the issue:

> Can anything fall more directly within the police power and internal regulation of a state than that which concerns the care and management of paupers, of convicts, or any other class or description of persons that may be thrown into the country, and likely to endanger its safety, or become chargeable for their maintenance? It is not intended by this remark to cast any reproach upon foreigners who may arrive in this country. But if all power to guard against these mischiefs is taken away, the safety and welfare of the community may be very much endangered.[7]

Violations of the laws by illegal aliens—starting with their initial violation of U.S. immigration legislation, and extending almost in a chain reaction to fraud and violation of federal, state, and local laws in many other areas—can only encourage disrespect for the law generally. Some of the advocacy groups that defend illegal immigration seek to excuse the violation of immigration law by holding up our immigration legislation as somehow "immoral," and by claiming that the economic and political conditions in the immigrant's country of origin justify seeking refuge and work in the United States illicitly. Such groups would also condone that attitude on the ground that the authorities in the immigrant's country of origin are repressive, conditioning the would-be illegal immigrant to distrust all authority; so encouraged, many illegals develop an attitude of defiance for authority and disregard the law after reaching the United States. But justification of such attitudes can only engender lawlessness on an ever greater scale, and ultimately undermine the rule of law that distinguishes American democracy from systems which deny democracy.

The threat of illegal immigration to the U.S. legal system also encourages violence and defiance towards U.S. officials and agencies —such as the INS, Drug Enforcement Administration, Customs Service, and local police—particularly in Mexico-U.S. border areas. Though his plight is emotionally wrenching, since the average illegal alien is desperate to reach a country where he can reasonably expect to find food, shelter, and personal security, a general attitude of antagonism towards U.S. law enforcement agencies—especially the INS, which is contemptuously called "*La Migra*"—can only foster banditry and violence by criminals against the illegals themselves, particularly in the act of crossing the border. Such criminals may often as not be illegal immigrants, too, or residents of Mexican border towns who prey on illegal immigrants, according to a study edited by Arthur F. Corwin.[8]

Unfortunately, the disrespect for the law and the threat to the U.S. legal system generally that stem from illegal immigration are encouraged, to some extent, by the supporters of illegal immigration into this country. Among them are certain immigrant advocacy organizations, church groups, immigration lawyers, and others who, by attacking our immigration laws as "invalid" or "socially unjust," only serve as false role models for their illegal immigrant clientele.

The long-term danger is that illegals who look up to such false role models may come to believe that, in general, violating the law is the way to get ahead in the United States. If that became the universal trend among illegals, it could eat away at the very foundations of American society.

5

The Burden on Social Services and Public Assistance

ALMOST HIDDEN away in its Metro section, the *Washington Post* published a poignant story headlined:

SCORES OF ARLANDRIA HISPANICS, FAR FROM HOME, NOW HOMELESS
After Losing Their Jobs, Men Are Begging, Sleeping on the Street

The story, appearing on March 16, 1991, reported that 50 to 100 Hispanic males between the ages of 18 and 40 had been thrown out of work and were living on the streets of Arlandria, an Alexandria, Virginia, community. Civic leaders, it went on, "are seeking expanded services to cope with what they describe as a growing problem that surfaced about six months ago," involving widespread unemployment in Northern Virginia due to the general recession. But unfortunately, Alexandria "is strapped for cash."

The *Post* reporter, Pierre Thomas, added that "matters are further complicated by cultural and language barriers," then explained:

> Some men in this group are not American citizens and do not have legal resident status, making them ineligible for many federal welfare programs. Many want help, but are wary of seeking government assistance because they fear it may lead to deportation, city officials say.[1]

How many of Arlandria's 2,325 Hispanics, out of a total population of 5,335, were illegals, the story did not venture to calculate. It broadly hinted at their status, however, that "some of these [homeless] people are in almost chronic underground status."[2]

Consequently, they avoid city shelters and must rely on support networks, often "staying with family members in over-crowded apartments." During the day they beg on the streets, creating an image of harsh poverty in a city generally considered affluent and attractive to tourists and other outsiders because of its considerable beauty and historical importance.

This vignette of social blight associated with illegal immigration may be relatively minor compared with what is happening in the Southwest and some major northern cities, but it reflects a persistent penetration of traditional American communities.

Typically, Arlandria's homeless Hispanics avoided seeking official relief for as illegals they belonged, as we have noted, to a growing underclass which generally shuns contact with officialdom. Studies bear out the fact that they make little use of income transfer programs such as Aid to Families with Dependent Children (AFDC), and food stamps, simply because they fear discovery of their illegal status. But as they acquire "street smarts," and learn to use the resources of networks and advocacy groups, they grow more confident in applying for aid.

As early as 1979, a survey of illegal aliens who had been living in Los Angeles for a long time and among whom there was a heavier presence of spouses and children, confirmed this trend. It showed an 8.9 percent participation rate in welfare programs, with 18.5 percent of the women reporting receipt of welfare payments, according to a study by M. D. Van Arsdol and others.[3] Professor David Heer, in a study of illegal aliens who gave birth in Los Angeles County hospitals, found that 19 percent were current recipients of food stamps. George J. Borjas, in an article in the *Wall Street Journal,* reported:

> Although the conventional wisdom is that immigrants shy away from welfare, the facts are quite different. Both immigrants and natives became more prone to take welfare in the 1970s, but the rate of increase was much faster for immigrants than for natives.... By 1980, immigrants were more

likely than natives to take welfare: 8.8 percent of immigrant households as against 7.9 percent of native.[4]

Legal and regulatory bars to illegal aliens' use of welfare have been inconsistent, shifting, and riddled with exceptions, and are frequently reshaped by court decisions. Thus:

• Illegal aliens are denied AFDC and food stamps, but pro-rata amounts of such aid can be allocated for use by their U.S. citizen children living among them.

• Congress forbade public housing assistance to illegal aliens in 1981, but because of litigation and Congressional second thoughts the implementing regulations were not initiated until 1988. The Housing and Community Development Act passed in 1987 gave local housing authorities the option of allowing illegal aliens to remain in public housing, to avoid dividing families, or to allow them an extensive period to seek alternative, affordable housing.

• Medicaid, the nation's $80-billion-a-year medical welfare program, is open to illegal aliens who are pregnant, disabled, or require emergency care. In a 1986 decision (*Lewis v. Gross*), the Federal District Court of New York held that illegal aliens are entitled to Medicaid because the federal Medicaid statute did not explicitly exclude them.

• The judicial concept of "Permanent Resident Alien under Color of Law," or "PRUCOL," has expanded the access of illegal aliens to welfare and public services. This doctrine holds that an illegal immigrant is *lawfully* present and is therefore entitled to public assistance unless the INS is actively seeking to deport him. Hundreds of thousands of aliens who remain under "deferred voluntary departure," or whose deportations are stayed while they legitimize their immigration status, are covered under "PRUCOL," report Daniel Stein and Steven Zanowic.[5]

• Illegal alien workers in such industries as California's perishable crop agriculture have been heavy users of unemployment compensation because of the inherent instability of seasonal farmwork, according to a report by David North.[6] New legislation and regulations now bar illegals from receiving unemployment payments. But in 1989, the California legislature passed a law excusing formerly illegal aliens who had received amnesty from repaying unemployment compensation received while in illegal status.

Probably the biggest single public assistance cost for illegal aliens is primary and secondary schooling. A watershed in the ongoing debate over the entitlements of illegal aliens was reached in the 1982 Supreme Court decision, *Doe v. Plyler*, which overturned a Texas law barring illegal immigrant children from free public education.

It is estimated that 3 to 5 million persons have remained in the United States illegally since the 1986 amnesty. Family data on legalized aliens show that about 14 percent of that population would be of school age (5 to 19 years), or 560,000 to 700,000 public school users. Using an average annual per pupil cost for U.S. public schools of $4,800, the total cost to taxpayers would be $2.7 billion to $3.4 billion. School nutrition programs and bilingual education add further costs whose totals are impossible to estimate but would clearly run high.

Confused policies, inconsistent laws, and generous court decisions on the rights of illegals have added up to a major burden on state and local public services and assistance budgets, particularly in low-income areas of the Southwest:

• In Los Angeles County "the costs of services provided to undocumented aliens continue to escalate," according to an official report by the County's Chief Administrative Officer, Richard B. Dixon. "The estimated net cost to the County grew. . . from 207.2 million in 1989-90 to $276.2 million in 1990-1991,"[7] it calculated. A second report by Dixon, on the Federal Government's share of the cost, noted that it had "increased from $57.7 million in 1989-90 to $140.5 million in 1990-91, and could reach $533 million by the year 2000."[8]

- Educating illegal alien children in the Los Angeles Unified School District costs $500 million a year, and is increasing by an estimated 20 percent annually.[9]

- Nearly 5,000 students in the Brownsville, Texas, independent school district are illegal aliens, many of whom commute illegally from Matamoros, directly across the border. Enrollment in the impoverished district is increasing by about 1,000 a year.[10]

- A neighboring Texas community, Hidalgo County, reported even more rapid growth of enrollments by illegal aliens from Mexico — a doubling of them in the first half of the 1980s.[11]

- In a Brooklyn school district known as the "United Nations of Immigrants," just one bilingual class serves 2,400 non-English speaking children.[12]

- Public hospitals in the Southwest have felt intense stress. Between 1983 and 1989, unreimbursed health care to illegal aliens cost Los Angeles County $778.8 million. In 1986, it cost much smaller El Paso $10 million for the care of indigent illegals at its Thomason General Hospital; it billed the Federal government but could not collect.[13]

- California Medicaid administrators are struggling with the problem of "illegal" illegal aliens. They are residents of Mexico who cross the border to receive subsidized medical assistance, show false documents proving that they are illegal alien "residents" of California, then become eligible for Medicaid. Providing Medicaid coverage to illegal aliens cost California $300 million in 1989.[14]

• In 1990, the welfare rolls in 49 states increased, due to the recession and the efforts of state governments to supply the needy with food, cash, and medical care. One reason for the welfare increase was, "changes in the immigration law [which] allowed more non-citizens onto the welfare rolls, an especially important factor in California and the Southwest."[15]

Confirming these experiences, Lief Jensen found in 1988 that the foreign born, according to U.S. Census data, were 56 percent more likely than natives to be in poverty, 25 percent more likely to receive public assistance and to have an average per capita income from public assistance 13.6 percent higher than natives.[16]

***

Why shouldn't federal, state, and local agencies foot the bill for the health, education, and welfare of illegals, as long as they pay their taxes? The question is, do they pay taxes as a rule? If so, do they pay *all* the taxes that would normally fall upon citizens or legal alien residents of the communities in which they live?

California's Health and Welfare Agency published *A Survey of Newly Legalized Persons in California,* in 1989, which reported public assistance use by former illegal aliens amnestied under IRCA, as follows:

Public Assistance Use by Former Illegal Aliens

Program	% Using
Unemployment Insurance	14.9
Workmen's Compensation	6.7
Women, Infants, Children (WIC)	32.7
State General Assistance	4.3

Program	% Using
Supplemental Security Income (SSI)	1.9
Welfare (AFDC)	4.4
Food Stamps	9.5

It is argued, by those who believe that illegal immigration carries little or no cost to the U.S. taxpayer, that illegals pay the taxes that fund the costs of public services to them. A major study in 1985 of Mexican aliens in Southern California, many of them illegal, analyzed extensively their contributions in state and local taxes and compared them to the total costs of state and local services they obtained. The study, done by Thomas Muller and Thomas J. Espenshade, found that Mexican immigrant households received $2,200 more in state and local services, including education, than they paid in taxes.[17]

Given the poor economic circumstances of illegal aliens generally, it is hard to see how their taxpaying ability could match, much less exceed the costs of services rendered to them. A person's capacity to pay taxes depends ultimately on his earnings ability. Illegal aliens are concentrated in low-wage, unstable occupations and tend to work fewer hours a year than the population as a whole. Obviously, low wages mean a low state and local income tax liability.

Although illegals often pay Social Security (FICA) taxes, those with children who are at or near the poverty level have their contributions rebated through earned income tax credits. Further, the indications are that tax compliance among illegals is lower than for the general population. North and Houston's 1976 survey of illegal alien workers shows that 22.7 percent of them did not have Social Security taxes withheld, 26.8 percent did not have federal income tax withheld, and 68.5 percent did not file federal income tax returns. Subsequently, in a 1989 study of GAO data on non-compliance of the foreign born with labor and tax laws, immigration researcher David North found that 44 percent of illegal aliens had received wage payments in cash, indicating the likelihood of non-payment of income tax and Social Security contributions.[18]

According to George J. Borjas:

> National income and tax revenues are substantially lower than they would have been if the U.S. had attracted more skilled immigrants. If the people who immigrated in the late 1970s had been as skilled as those who came in the early 1960s, national income would be at least $6 billion higher and tax revenues would have increased by $1.5 billion per year.[19]

***

The classic argument in favor of unrestricted immigration into the United States, whether legal or illegal, is that the country needs workers able and willing to perform tasks that American citizens are unwilling to perform and at lower wages but the same level of efficiency.

That is not necessarily true. Various observers have noted that Americans and legal aliens will accept a variety of low-paying jobs. In Houston, for example, former INS District Director Paul B. O'Neill, related during an interview: "There are thousands and thousands of jobs American citizens would take [if illegal aliens did not compete for them]."[20] So would legal aliens.

As a concrete instance, in 1986 O'Neill's staff investigators apprehended 69 illegals working for a janitorial service which was contracted to clean prestigious office buildings in downtown Houston. Within three days, he reported, 130 U.S. citizens and legal aliens applied for the vacated janitorial jobs.

In any event, immigration scholars who have examined data on the foreign-born over the last two decades have found evidence of a significant decline in the labor-market performance, competitiveness, and educational achievements of immigrants, along with a rising incidence of poverty and greater use of income transfer and public assistance programs. Borjas found, upon examining 1970 and 1980 census data, that immigrants are 15.2 percent more likely to be in poverty, 6.1 percent to suffer unemployment, and 13.8 percent to be on welfare.[21]

In his latest book, *A Marriage of Convenience: Relations Between Mexico and the United States*, Sidney Weintraub corroborated the findings of Borjas and others who hold that today's immigrants, particularly Mexicans, are relatively unskilled and have little education. He writes:

> Recent immigrants tend to come with fewer skills and fewer years schooling that did earlier ones, and their economic progress may not prove to be comparable. This is particularly true of Mexican immigrants, who have an average of 7.5 years of schooling, compared with more than 11 years for other Hispanics and whites.[22]

Weintraub adds that "the illegality of undocumented immigrant settlers makes their economic progress problematic," but qualifies his statement with the caution that "precise time-series data are not readily available as a consequence of the illegality."

The trends contrast starkly with the popular view of the immigrant as an energetic self-starter who displays a high degree of upward mobility after resettlement in his new land. That appears no longer to be true, except where some recent Asian and Soviet Jewish arrivals are concerned.

Borjas and University of Chicago social scientist Barry Chiswick attribute the declining quality of immigrants to a weakening of the process for selecting immigrants. In the 1960s, 1970s, and 1980s, ever larger proportions of new arrivals in this country were refugees or illegal aliens who are not subject to the immigration law's requirements for screening for labor market adaptability or likelihood of becoming a public charge.[23]

The illegal immigrant stream into the United States, which adds about 250,000 to 300,000 new permanent settlers each year, is predominantly Mexican, disproportionately undereducated and unskilled, and almost totally non-English speaking. These disabilities are major handicaps in securing steady, well-paid jobs. In many instances, they are a virtual prescription for poverty.

The make-up of the Mexican illegal alien influx has changed over time; a tendency to require public assistance, for example, is on the rise. Earlier waves were composed largely of young male workers under thirty years of age. In later waves, they were joined by spouses and children and even aged parents, a population with far greater need for services such as health care, schools and food stamps, as North showed in his study on the *Impact of Legal, Illegal and Refugee Migrations on U.S. Social Service Programs*.

The U.S. Government has constructed an extensive and costly social and economic safety net, over the past half-century, for the less fortunate members of the national community whose interests it exists to serve. Illegal immigration may threaten the viability and solvency of that safety net and the concept of community underlying it. The primary obligation of the nation-state is to its legitimate citizens and legal residents. The concept of community becomes hollow if outsiders can enter it in defiance of its laws and regulations, and swiftly gain entitlements to its benefits. The very viability of the U.S. welfare system is threatened when resources for the neediest are diluted by the claims of outsiders, and taxpayers conclude that the number of potential claimants is not limited by national boundaries.

6

The Effect on the Labor Market

WHAT EFFECT is illegal immigration having on America? On its cities? On its labor market? On its school and health facilities? Does illegal immigration, for example, take away jobs from American and legal foreign workers in the United States? Or does it, rather, result in the creation of new jobs?

Before trying to answer these and related questions, let us first discuss the likely projections of future illegal immigration. Most immigration experts seem to agree that the trend is toward higher immigration, in general, overwhelmingly from Mexico but also from Central America, and that it will persist throughout the rest of the century. Sidney Weintraub, who is well known for his sympathetic attitude toward Mexico's problems, particularly immigration, collaborated with Chandler Stolp in a study which "sought to project Mexican economic migration to the United States to the year 2000." They concluded that ". . . . it would be unwise to anticipate an easing of immigration pressure over this period regardless of the international economic setting."[1]

Weintraub, using projections made by the Mexican Government's Department of Programming and Budget, calculated that Mexico's economically active population by the year 2000 would total between 35 and 40 million. It presently stands at about 30 million. He doubts seriously that Mexico can supply jobs for an estimated "oversupply" of 5.6 million or more workers. The pressure to emigrate to El Norte, he again concludes, "is unlikely to abate for at least the rest of this century."[2]

47

This means that the U.S. labor pool will probably be augmented by an ever-growing number of illegals, probably running into the millions, and that native and legal foreign workers will be adversely affected. Studies show that the unchecked growth of illegal immigration into the United States could threaten the equilibrium of the labor market in certain major urban areas. The presence in any area of substantial numbers of illegals is usually accompanied by depressed wages, particularly in the vicinity of the border. They are willing and able to work for the minimum wage or less, and since they fear detection by the authorities they are unlikely to blow the whistle on unscrupulous employers who refuse to pay more. They have a competitive edge over U.S. or legal foreign workers because, in many cases, they are unmarried or have dependents in Mexico whose support costs and expectations are lower.

A major study made by the Department of Labor in 1989,[3] while lauding the many positive contributions of immigrants, took note of a series of adverse labor market effects found in previous studies, such as:

• Where wages are concerned, arriving immigrants have the greatest effects on the earnings of earlier immigrants: a 10 percent increase in the numbers of new immigrants decreases the average wage of foreign-born workers by between 2 and 9 percent.

• An increase in the supply of immigrants may extend the period that unemployed workers must search for jobs.

• The effects of Mexican immigration on Los Angeles are generally benign, but its probable effects on the Hispanic labor force—especially on recent arrivals with similar characteristics—are somewhat less so. Research in Southern California suggests that immigrants have a dampening effect on wages in selected industries requiring low skills.

• The deteriorating economic condition of Texans of Mexican origin during the 1970s possibly resulted from the influx of large numbers of Mexican immigrants. On the border, the probable impact of commuter workers from Mexico was to displace some agricultural workers and to depress wages in a loose labor market.

• The shoe industry's survival in Southern California appears tied to low-paid legal and illegal Mexican workers. Jobs are unstable, and offer poor compensation besides. There seems to be no mechanism for bringing in domestic workers.

• The meat packers' solution to controlling wage costs clearly included recruiting immigrants, which have displaced many American workers, including blacks.

• Because of competition by non-union firms employing immigrant workers, the number of unionized black janitors in Los Angeles dropped from 2,500 in 1977 to 600 in 1985.

• In New York, the shift of business to smaller construction firms using immigrant labor has weakened the role of black workers in the industry.

• In agriculture, the continued availability of new immigrant workers weakens the demand for domestic workers and established immigrants. Farm workers outnumber available jobs by nearly two to one. Some farmers hire as many as ten times the number of workers needed, simply to maintain one complete harvest crew.

• Three key effects of immigrant labor on the California fruit and vegetable industry are a retardation of mechanization, a reduction in responsiveness to consumer tastes, the inflation of land values.

• As the immigrants' expectations of better working conditions begin to match those of the native work force, settled immigrants may find themselves displaced by new arrivals. The citrus and furniture-manufacturing industries are pertinent examples.

• The reliance of immigrant entrepreneurs on the labor of co-ethnics isolates ethnic firms from general labor market forces, including pressures for unionization, and reduces the need for strict adherence to labor regulations.

Los Angeles is a prime example of labor markets disrupted by immigration, the Labor Department study found. Other studies, like that of Muller and Espenshade, indicate that, as large numbers of illegal aliens (mainly from Mexico) move into the Greater Los Angeles area, the tendency is for both black and non-Hispanic white workers to move out.

Borjas and Marta Tienda confirmed in their study, *The Economic Consequences of Immigration*, that illegals had practically no effect upon the wages of native workers but had a depressing effect upon those of fellow immigrants. In a separate account, Borjas concluded:

> A 10 percent increase in the number of immigrants decreases the average native wage by at most two-tenths of one percent, and has little effect on the unemployment rate of practically all native groups, including the black poor.[4]

Is the big influx of cheap and willing workers an asset, as some claim? Perhaps for employers, yes, but for blue collar workers, particularly blacks and Hispanics, it is bad news. In their study, *The Fourth Wave: California's Newest Immigrants*, Muller and Espenshade found:

> Relative average wages of unskilled workers in the Los Angeles manufacturing sector have declined dramatically — from 2 percent above the U.S. metropolitan average in 1969 and 1970 to 12 percent below the average a decade later.[5]

Considering the evidence of the Muller-Espenshade report on Mexican aliens in Southern California's labor market, former Secretary of Labor Ray Marshall concluded that

> if international migration had made no impact on local wages (as some economists argue), it is assumed that wage increases, on a percentage basis, would have been about the same for [Los Angeles] county as for the nation. This is clearly not the case in several sectors of the labor market where massive migration from Mexico (much of it illegal) depressed wages substantially.[6]

Julian L. Simon takes a different view. He argues, in general, that an "open border"—unlimited immigration—is good for the United States, particularly for its economy. He holds that

> general immigration causes little or no unemployment at large, even in the first year or two; the same is true of low-income Hispanic immigration even among the groups most likely to be 'displaced' by them.[7]

Simon states further: "Immigrants not only take jobs, they make jobs."[8] He acknowledges, however, that the impact of illegals on the American workforce is negative:

> First, the illegals, and especially those from Mexico, tend to have less education and less skill relative to legal immigrants. This means that they have a disproportionate negative effect on natives with low skills and education."[9]

Simon does not, however, favor reducing illegal migration. He believes that the problem "should be seen in the broad context of protection of all lower-skill groups threatened by imports and immigration."[10]

In an analysis he made in 1988, Secretary Marshall inferred from the large outmigration of native blue collar workers in the 1970s that, even though job creation remained high, substantial labor displacement by Mexican immigrants had occurred.

This is particularly so where black workers are concerned. Dr. Frank Morris, former Executive Director of the Congressional Black Caucus Foundation, gave a statement to the House of Representatives on March 13, 1990, that blacks were worried over the growth of the foreign-born population by some 750,000 annually. He explained the central reason for such concern:

> This remarkable growth of the immigrant population is most intense in areas where African-Americans have a major presence and have important interests.[11]

He added:

> It is clear that America's black population is bearing a disproportionate share of immigrants' competition for jobs, housing and social services. While each year's immigrant cohort brings the nation some needed technical and professional skills, illegal immigration . . . yields a sizable and growing segment of immigrants whose educational deficiencies and low skills parallel those of many black Americans who are struggling to rise out of poverty.[12]

Of course all the adverse conditions noted above worsened as recession struck the United States in 1990, and millions of Americans were thrown out of work. Most frightening to the newly unemployed was that some, perhaps many, of them might never recover their old jobs because companies had learned to do with fewer hands. This was a result of achieving greater efficiency in the workplace or of the adoption of machine-intensive technology, or the need to meet sharpening competition from abroad.

***

Exploitation of illegal immigrants by unscrupulous U.S. employers, which has proceeded apace ever since illegal immigration became common in the 1920s, has only exacerbated competition for jobs. The very status of being undocumented makes an immigrant vulnerable to exploitation. Employers in agriculture, industry, or the service sector are naturally prone to use illegal immigrants as a source of cheap labor who often perform menial work—e.g., dishwashing — that native-born or legal alien workers are not willing to at the depressed wages and conditions that prevail.

Employers of illegal immigrants can usually obtain these advantages: 1) pay minimal wages (at best the federal minimum wage, frequently less); 2) evade remitting Federal or Social Security taxes on employees; 3) evade legal mandatory safety, health, and other labor standards whenever they can, and 4) get more work out of illegals because they dare not complain to the authorities about unfair treatment.

Employer exploitation of illegal aliens, abetted by their increasing numbers in the United States, has even led to the resurgence on a large scale of classic "sweatshops." To cite one example of the flagrant abuse and exploitation of illegal immigrant child labor, Michael Powell provides this graphic description of a New York City immigrant sweatshop:

> On the 12th floor of 333 West 39th street, [a 15-year-old boy] works in conditions considered barbaric half a century ago. [He] could be found by his table. . . sewing pleats into cheap white chiffon skirts. He hopes to make $1.00 an hour, even as winter winds whirl through a picture-window size hole in the back wall and take all feeling from his fingers. The temperature outside is 8 degrees. Fluffy blue ear muffs frame this Mexican immigrant's face and he wears a thin cloth jacket, slacks, scuffed loafers and a scared look. 'I can't lose my job, [the boy] pleads in a monotone whisper in Spanish to an inspector from the state Department of Labor. 'We have no money.'[13]

The exploitation of illegal immigrants by U.S. employers has on occasion even enjoyed semi-legitimate status. The Immigration and Nationality Act of 1952 contained a loophole known as the "Texas Proviso," which enabled employers of illegals to evade the law. The Act made it illegal for undocumented aliens to enter the United States and made them subject to deportation if caught, but it did not make it unlawful for employers to knowingly hire illegal aliens nor penalize them for having illegal immigrants in their employ. A subsection of Section 274 of the Immigration and Nationality Act made it a felony, subject to a $ 2,000-dollar fine and/ or a five-year prison term, for, *inter alia*, "harboring" illegal aliens. But it added, "Provided, however, that for the purposes of this section, employment (including the usual and normal practices incident to employment) shall not be deemed to constitute harboring"[14]—this was the Texas Proviso.

The Texas Proviso was inserted into the Act at the insistence of agricultural employers in Texas and other states of the Southwest.

They had always employed large numbers of illegal aliens because they worked for less than others, and they did not want this source of cheap labor to be interrupted. So, as Paul R. Ehrlich reported in his study,[15] they had their powerful lobby in Washington put through the Texas Proviso. Though inconsistent with our immigration legislation, it provided quasi-legal encouragement to illegal immigration for more than thirty years, until 1986, when the Immigration Reform and Control Act was passed.

From the early 1970s, many efforts were made to enact legislation providing for sanctions against employers who knowingly hired illegal aliens. Those efforts were strongly supported by the American trade union movement as well as by various other organizations. It was only with the passage of IRCA, however, and after more than a dozen states had already adopted similar legislation, that employer sanctions were finally enacted into federal law. The 1986 Act imposed upon employers the requirement that they verify the immigration status of job applicants before hiring them, involving completion of a Form I-9 combined with documentary proof of immigration or citizenship status. This "employer sanctions" provision of IRCA was adopted in conjunction with the Act's amnesty feature, which granted 3.1 million illegal aliens who had arrived in the United States prior to 1980 the opportunity to legalize their status and remain in the country as legal residents.[16] Most of them—2.3 million, about 75 percent—were listed by INS as Mexicans.

Some Hispanic and other ethnic advocacy groups have, since the passage of IRCA, mounted a strong campaign to get the Act's employer sanctions feature revoked by Congress. They hold that it permits employers to deny work to anyone who is "foreign looking" or has a foreign accent, and hence encourages discrimination against permanent resident aliens and U.S. citizens of Hispanic and other ethnic backgrounds.

The third and final report on sanctions by the General Accounting Office, issued in April 1990, indirectly acknowledged that discrimination existed, when it concluded that it "could be reduced if employers were provided with more education on the law's requirements and a simpler and more reliable verification system."[17] Most employers seemed to agree, pointing out that they are confused at having to deal with 17 different documents which may be involved in proving identity and work authorization. The GAO report disclosed that 461,000 employers were discriminating based on "foreign" appearance or accent, while 346,000 unlawfully requested work documentation only of persons with "foreign" characteristics.

On the other hand, the GAO reported that sanctions "[have] apparently reduced illegal immigration and [are] not an unnecessary burden on employers."[18] Some Hispanic leaders agree, and strongly support maintenance of IRCA's employer sanctions provision. Ricardo Estrada, an immigration expert who writes a column for the *Dallas Morning News*, argues at the same time against the "grandfathering" of illegals who arrived in the United States before 1982. Estrada, whose own grandparents were born in Mexico, is quoted by fellow-columnist William Raspberry in the *Washington Post* as asserting:

> Those two provisions [in IRCA] make it a very schizophrenic, very ambivalent attempt at immigration reform, because it threatens simply to regularize the influx, which in any case will still have a negative economic impact on Hispanic citizens. A straight sanctions provision, bereft of the amnesty and farm workers' provisions [which permit seasonal farm workers into the country legally], would have done the most good.[19]

Polls taken of Hispanics reveal that they overwhelmingly support employer sanctions. One conducted by the V. Lance Tarrance and Peter D. Hart organizations, sponsored by the pro-sanctions Federation for American Immigration Reform, found that Hispanics support sanctions by nearly 2-1. It reported that 60 percent of both black and Hispanic respondents favored sanctions.

Still, some Congressional leaders have sponsored joint resolutions to eliminate sanctions from IRCA. A bill co-sponsored by Sens. Orrin Hatch (R-UT) and Edward Kennedy (D-MA) in the Senate, and Rep. Edward Roybal (D-CA) in the House, would repeal employer sanctions but also increase penalties for harboring or smuggling illegal aliens and strengthen the Border Patrol.

Employers who exploit illegal immigrants are not exclusively long-time citizens or of non-Hispanic origin. Among the worst exploiters have been erstwhile illegal immigrants themselves. Some of the most inhumane abuses of illegals occur in agriculture, where illegal immigrant seasonal and non-seasonal agricultural workers are usually under the supervision and control of a "crew chief" or labor contractor (who also is frequently the person who recruits them as well). He may be a national of the same country as the illegal workers, may also be illegal, and is often found to engage in some of the crasser kinds of exploitation and abuse, Corwin has reported.[20]

Employers are by no means the only class which exploits illegal immigrants. The illegals' status outside the law, their traditionally docile and uncomplaining attitude, and their fear of the direst consequences if they seek help from the authorities, leave them open to exploitation by all sorts of people who lack scruples. After employers, perhaps the class with the next highest incidence of abuse of illegals is landlords. They will house illegals, as a rule, under the most unhealthy conditions, in crowded and unsanitary apartments, shanties, garages, tool sheds, whatever can be considered shelter, however primitive. To boot, they tend to charge the poorest immigrants exorbitant rents.

**

A strange, but not necessarily unique example of illegals entrapped in what might be called "white collar crime" came to light in the nation's capital in December 1990, when a bank called the "Latin Investment Corporation" went bankrupt. The Latin Investment Corporation had been operating in the District of Columbia as a bank though it had no banking charter. Its clientele consisted almost entirely of *latinos*, predominantly Salvadorans, who had entered the country illegally; they entrusted their savings in the care of LIC because its president, Fernando Leonzo, was of the same nationality and originally an illegal immigrant himself. They were able to make deposits in Latin Investment Corporation because, unlike chartered banks, it did not require depositors to show Social Security or other documentation proving that they were legitimate. It was totally unregulated and operated outside the banking laws of the District.

When Leonzo's financial operation collapsed in December 1990, it left penniless some 3,000 clients, the great majority of whom were illegals; they lost nearly all of their $6.5 million in deposits.

Leonzo, with no law to restrain him, had felt free to invest their money in real estate, the purchase of homes for bank officers, a Latin newspaper, and other projects which consistently yielded a loss. In the process, he acquired great local prestige as a pillar of the Hispanic community. When questioned by irate customers in the U.S. District Court's hearing room to tell them what had happened to their money, he answered with aplomb:

"It was never our intention to take your money."

Though he admitted that he had used his immigrant depositors' savings to invest in other business enterprises, Leonzo was unable to remember how much Latin Investment Corporation had lent those businesses or how much, if any, of the loaned money had been repaid.

Lawyers for the defrauded depositors held out little hope that they would ever see their money again. Unfortunately, they have no legal redress, for they do not dare appear in a court suit as long as they are undocumented aliens. They are simply persons without legal rights.

***

Though only indirectly related to the LIC case, illegal immigration distorts investment and business decisions. Economist Vernon Briggs notes that illegal immigration shapes labor markets as well as responds to them. Aliens do come where the jobs are, but in many instances jobs go where the aliens are. Thus decisions by business to invest and establish factories in parts of the United States inhabited by masses of illegal immigrant labor often appear to be based largely on the availability of a cheap, docile, and readily exploitable illegal immigrant labor force.

Not a few factories in cities close to the border, principally in the south of California and of Texas, were established there (sometimes re-locating from other parts of the United States) primarily to take advantage of the cheap labor afforded by the presence of great numbers of illegal aliens. But the availability of cheap immigrant labor as a basis for making decisions on investment is shortsighted and, in the long run, inimical to a sound and competitive U.S. economy.

Agricultural economist Philip Martin describes how the availability of cheap illegal farm labor in California is an implicit subsidy to California's perishable crop farms in the same sense that federally subsidized water for irrigation is. One of the chief costs in such businesses is wages, and low immigrant wages are soon factored into the prices of land and business assets. Fifty years ago, the lack of water and labor uncertainties made much of the Southwest's farmland almost worthless. However, federal irrigation projects and Mexican farm workers have made southwestern farmland some of the most valuable in the United States.

Despite IRCA's reforms, and the requirements of the Migrant and Seasonal Workers Protection Act enforced by the Department of Labor, illegal alien workers and abuse of them are still common in agriculture. Farm worker wages have remained stagnant since the 1986 reforms. Such practices by labor contractors as wage trimming, sale of alcoholic beverages, and failure to meet health and safety standards, are rife.

Philip Martin concludes:

> Some of the service establishments, factories, and farms of the most sophisticated economy in the world are dependent on the most remote Mexican or Central American villages for unskilled labor. These dependencies are distorting economic development in both the United States and Mexican economies; the U.S. economy is importing large numbers of workers, along with goods and capital, despite unemployment of about seven percent and idle industrial capacity; Mexico is allowing the export of workers to the United States, thus increasing its dependency on and vulnerability to the U.S. of its own capital-intensive industries.[21]

Former Secretary of Labor Ray Marshall sees illegal immigration as distorting investment decisions and labor allocation:

> In fact, illegal immigration restructures the very nature of the local and the national economy, distorting, for example, the investment decisions made in labor-intensive industries such as garments, tilting investment toward Los Angeles and away from the rest of the country. In the short run, the winners would seem to be the Los Angeles factory owners who are

getting the de facto wage subsidies from the presence of the undocu-
menteds; but in the long run the situation does not bode well for healthy
economic growth in the nation, the state of California, the county of Los
Angeles and perhaps even in the firms now relying on the illegal immigrants. These investment decisions retain, temporarily, some marginal
low wage jobs in the United States that otherwise might disappear or move
to the Third World. The alternatives, if there are economic reasons for
having these jobs in the United States, would be to raise wages, improve
management or to mechanize.

It is very unrealistic to assume that the United States can compete in
even minimum wage jobs in those products where wages constitute the
principal source of competitive advantage. The only hope for
competitiveness in the international market on terms that will maintain
American living standards is to improve productivity and quality through
mechanization, skill upgrading or improved management and production
systems, all of which are discouraged by a steady flow of illegal, low-wage
migrants.[22]

7

The Increase in Border Violence

VULNERABLE TO exploitation by unscrupulous employers and landlords in the United States, the illegal immigrant is actually open to victimization long before he gets there. He becomes a potential victim the moment he decides to leave his *pueblo* to make the arduous trek northward — the moment, that is, when he opts to do so illicitly, without proper documentation.

An illegal immigrant runs the risk of being victimized when, as a first step, he seeks the aid of a coyote — a Mexican smuggler — to get him across the Río Grande. Or, alternately, when he is approached by a narcotics trafficker, who may be the same coyote in another guise, and who can also get him across and *pay him money in the bargain*, if only he will carry over a packet of cocaine or heroin. (The smuggled substance is to be passed on, of course, to a drug courier waiting on the U.S. side.) The chance to make some money, even though unlawfully, can be too tempting to refuse.

Such arrangements with smugglers and other criminals contain the seeds of self-destruction for an illegal migrant. They can, at the very least, prove hazardous. They might lead to apprehension by the U.S. Customs Service or Border Patrol, and jail. If there is resistance, violence could ensue, and the lives of both illegal immigrant and law enforcement officer will be at stake.

The potential for violence is ever present in the life of an illegal immigrant. Once he decides to head for El Norte surreptitiously he becomes, willy nilly, an outlaw. He lays his life on the line and is fair game for criminals or, on the other hand, he chances a rough encounter with the authorities.

Much of the time, violence occurs even before the would-be illegal immigrant leaves Mexico. A coyote is the principal danger to be faced. For a fee ranging from a few hundred to a thousand dollars or more, the coyote will arrange to smuggle a Mexican worker across the border, usually along with others seeking the same assistance. For a larger fee, he will promise to put them up in safehouses on the U.S. side, transport them to their ultimate U.S. destinations, or even place them in jobs. On the other hand, a coyote may decide to rob a prospective illegal immigrant at the first opportunity, while still on the Mexican side of the border; if he resists, the coyote is quite capable of maiming or killing him and leaving him in the gutter in a town where he is utterly unknown. In fact, the majority of documented incidents of violence along our southern border are committed in Mexico by Mexican nationals against unwitting immigrants. The most frequent offenders are the coyotes, who are usually based in a Mexican border town.

The coyote is ideally positioned to prey on the illegal immigrant, who is virtually at the criminal's mercy. He is in a strange town without relatives or friends, he is ignorant of the surroundings, he does not know how to gain access to the U.S. side, he has no idea of where he will go if he gets there, or how. He only knows fear — fear of the *policía* — of both countries. He must perforce rely upon someone who is familiar with the obstacles to be encountered and how to overcome them: the coyote. The latter, though, too often turns out to be no friend. In company with other border bandits, he is as likely as not to force his helpless illegal client to part with his funds, his jewelry, and other valuables before or after crossing into the United States.

Gangs of coyotes think nothing, either, of raping female illegals while robbing them and their men. Nor, for that matter, of killing them should they resist extortion, robbery or rape, or out of simple vengeance, according to Arthur Corwin.[1]

A case study done by Daniel Wolf, in 1988, quotes the San Diego Deputy Police Chief as complaining about

> the problem of undocumenteds robbing, raping, and murdering other undocumenteds, who have cashed out their worldly possessions. Armed bandits lie waiting in bushes along common paths on their side [of the

border], stop them, and rob them, rape the women, and assault the men. There are about six to ten murders per year like this, and these go on our murder toll, though none are U.S. citizens.[2]

Instances of callous disregard of their fellow human beings by alien smugglers make newspaper headlines. (This is the case largely in the Southwest; the Eastern media pay little or no attention to border violence.) One especially grim incident took place in 1986, when 63 illegal aliens smuggled into the United States by a coyote were locked inside a railroad boxcar near Laredo, Texas, and abandoned by him. Two of the illegals in the boxcar died; the rest barely escaped death by suffocation when they were discovered and freed.[3] A similar horrifying incident occurred in 1986, when a coyote who escorted more than a dozen aliens on foot from Mexico into Arizona abandoned them in the desert, where they got lost; several of them died from heat exhaustion and exposure.

The countless thousands of illegal aliens who attempt to sneak across the border by themselves fare no better than the organized groups escorted by coyotes, and frequently they suffer even more. Aliens are more likely to be subjected to violence when crossing alone, running a greater risk of being raped, robbed, and murdered by the many criminals and marauding gangs mostly from the Mexican side of the Río Grande. Both sides of the border are filled with ravines, arroyos, rocks, and desert shrubs which afford ideal hiding places for predators intending to waylay defenseless individuals who happen to be crossing over on foot.

Sometimes illegal immigrants themselves will engage in violence against their fellow illegals, reports Wolf, and may continue to engage in criminal activities and violence once in the United States. Fortunately, these are in the distinct minority. The overwhelming majority of illegal aliens do not engage in violence or crime in the United States, and if they skirt the law because of their status they do not necessarily commit violent acts of lawlessness. The minority of illegal aliens in the United States who do so constitute, however, a disproportionately large, and growing, percentage of our prison and criminal population. Illustrating the crime threat posed by this minority, Gail Diane Cox, writing in the *Los Angeles Daily Journal* about an INS survey of the issue, reported:

Undocumented aliens make up about one fifth of the population of Los Angeles County's central jail, according to a new survey by the federal Immigration and Naturalization Service. Melvin Calvert, Deputy Assistant Regional Commissioner of the INS investigations program, said Wednesday that he analyzed those released from the jail on a single day. That data, along with background reports, show the county is spending about $90,000 a day to incarcerate foreign nationals arrested for assorted felonies and misdemeanors after entering the United States without inspection, Calvert said.

The jail, with about 8,500 prisoners, [is] the largest concentration of inmates in the nation.... The INS survey coincides with public complaints by a ranking member of the Los Angeles Police Department, that as much as half the downtown crime is attributable to undocumented aliens returned to the streets through bail and probation.[4]

Jerry Seper wrote a series of five descriptive articles for the *Washington Times* entitled, "America's Border War." In the final one, he was able to update and confirm Cox's earlier story, reporting as follows:

Los Angeles and other major cities say about a third of the major crimes reported each year may be attributable to illegal aliens. Others say the average is about 15 percent.[5]

Seper quoted an INS estimate that "there are more than 120,000 illegal aliens currently in federal, state, or local jails nationwide."

His conclusion:

Crimes committed annually by illegal aliens in the United States are skyrocketing, fueled in part, critics say, by an unwieldy and impractical deportation process.[6]

***

The truly frightening aspect of the illegal immigration across our southern border is that it tends to foster violence. For some years, even before the recent resurgence in illegal crossings, the increase in violence and the threat of it along the border have been such as to alarm law-abiding residents of the region. The Light Up the Border movement was one reflection of that concern. In some cases, citizens, including lawmakers, have demanded that Washington "militarize" the border to keep out illegals. But that is hardly feasible, and not at all likely to happen, as it would only cause a backlash among our Mexican neighbors and even among many Americans.

Some interest groups have charged that the violence is often caused or provoked by the U.S. Border Patrol, in an overzealous effort to enforce our immigration laws. But there are only 3,857 Border Patrol personnel, out of a grand total of 4,324, who are assigned to patrol the 9 Southwest sectors along 2,000 miles of border and they must cope with an upsurge in illegal crossings into the United States estimated at 3 to 5 million—some Border Patrol agents put the total

TABLE 2
Border Patrol Anti-Crime Activities 1984-1989

Mission	1984	1985	1986	1987	1988	1989
Alien smugglers arrested	13,435	14,666	19,275	11,560	10,373	13,794
Smuggler vehicles seized	6,456	7,327	10,307	7,512	6,643	10,789
Criminal aliens located	8,745	9,786	14,429	15,143	16,629	17,687
Narcotics seizures	1,501	2,457	3,481	5,392	5,824	8,756
Value of drugs seized ($ mil.)	54.4	130.1	264.2	661.7	803.5	1987.9

Source: INS Statistical Yearbook 1989

at 10 million—annually. In fact, the Border Patrol has 9 percent fewer agents than it did in 1988, according to a GAO study dated March 1991. And of those assigned to the Southwest border only 800 are on duty at any one time. "Further, the proportion of total Border Patrol agent time devoted to border control activities decreased from 71 percent to 60 percent from 1986 to 1990," continues the GAO study. Yet alien apprehensions, the GAO found, "were 23 percent higher than in fiscal year 1989."[7] The skimpy Border Patrol is far outnumbered by the aliens who attempt to steal across the Río Grande daily. (See Table 2.)

The busiest port of entry along the entire border is in the San Diego Sector at San Ysidro, California, just opposite Tijuana. Upwards of one million illegals cross here every year, of which perhaps one-third will be apprehended and deported to Mexico. Seper offers a graphic description of what happens in this sector:

> Some nights, as many as 1,000 [illegal aliens] mill about the top of the levee [on the Tijuana River one mile west of the border] waiting for a signal, usually about 3 a. m., to run en masse down the earthen embankment to the U.S. side.
>
> As few as six Border Patrol agents are stationed at the base of the levee, at intervals of about 100 yards. They man what the Patrol calls 'still watch positions,' and their job is to deter illegal immigration.
>
> The windows and lights on many of their pale-green trucks are encased in wire mesh to protect the agents from the hundreds of rocks, bottles and pieces of concrete thrown at them nightly. Coyotes devised the tactic to force agents to retreat.
>
> Sometimes, a group of as many as 100 illegal aliens will rush a single Border Patrol truck when they discover it is manned by a lone agent, forcing his retreat. Once the aliens break across the levee, they are in open field and headed north.[8]

Inevitably, there are cases of Border Patrol agents who have overstepped the bounds and used excessive force to apprehend illegals, and of course that is inexcusable. Some allegations of violence and undue use of force by agents do have a basis in fact, and appropriate investigations have been conducted and disciplinary and other actions taken. It would be unrealistic to expect that, given the impossible odds they must confront daily, the agents comport themselves like saints. Still, over the past two decades the Border Patrol appears to have gone to great lengths to avoid the use of undue force in apprehending illegal aliens crossing into the United States, and to have given its agents appropriate training in peaceful means of handling their difficult duties.

Much room for misunderstanding exists, as is true of police forces and other law-enforcement agencies throughout the United States. The potential for what could be construed as excessive use of force inheres in any situation involving apprehensions, night or day, of illegal aliens. This is particularly true when the primary objective of the illegal who is apprehended may be to break away and escape from the Border Patrol officers, even if he must use physical means to do so.

On the other hand, the potential for violence *against* members of the Border Patrol by illegal border crossers appears to have increased markedly in recent years. "[T]he Border Patrol has reported an increase since 1987 in assaults against its agents along the Southwest border," states the GAO study cited above. Since they are so few in number, "Border Patrol agents make few efforts to confront the illegal aliens near the border, considering the nearly 200 assaults and shootings in the past few months," reports Jerry Seper. The reason, of course, is that the Border Patrol is hopelessly undermanned and outnumbered by the massive numbers of illegals crossing the border. A single Border Patrol agent may often have to face, arrest, and escort a sizeable crowd of apprehended illegal aliens, as this writer can personally attest.

In sum, the atmosphere in some border areas, as symbolized by the Tijuana/San Diego no-man's-land of sinister canyons and ravines, is sometimes reminiscent of the Wild West. But unlike the old outlaws, the coyotes and other border smugglers who infest the region are highly mechanized. They use pickups and other motor vehicles to criss-cross the frontier on their nefarious errands, often forcing the Border Patrol to engage in dangerous high-speed chases after them.

Border violence had already become so general by the end of the 1970s that, in the San Diego area, the Border Patrol formed a special squad in cooperation with the San Diego police to counteract violence perpetrated against illegal immigrants by smugglers and other criminals. This anti-violence squad has achieved some success in combatting border violence, to the extent that it has won grudging praise from immigrant advocacy groups and others normally harshly critical of the Border Patrol. Nonetheless, its anti-violence, anti-crime effort has made only a dent in the problem, because it is so great, while the resources committed to handle it—such as the number of Border Patrol agents—are so small.

Meanwhile, the outlook is for even more violence on the Mexican-U.S. border in the foreseeable future, as the Seper series indicates. Not only is the number of illegals crossing on the increase, as we have noted more than once, but the number of underemployed young people grows. Then again, the border is becoming more urbanized, as is Mexico in general, changing radically the composition of the Mexican alien flow.

Today's arrivals come chiefly from Mexico's cities, not its rural areas, they are less docile and more aggressive, and they are more likely to have a criminal past and/or criminal records. More and more toughs from the streets of Tijuana, Juárez, and other Mexican border cities seem ready to stir up trouble wherever they can. Because of the prevalence of drug trafficking, they are also more likely to be armed. The Border Patrol, in cases where it is seriously outnumbered, has had to withdraw from areas where it is also outgunned. In the Nogales border area, for instance, U.S. Marine units had to be called in to aid in drug interdiction efforts in December 1989 and found themselves in a firefight with narcotics smugglers.

8

Illegals and the Drug Traffic

ILLEGAL IMMIGRATION into the United States has become a vital instrument used by both Mexican and Colombian drug smugglers to infiltrate increasing quantities of narcotics into this country, at a time when both the Mexican and U.S. governments are cooperating closely to win the drug war. In recent years, ever larger amounts of cocaine are being transported from Colombia to Mexico, then transshipped across the border; these are in addition to traditional Mexican-produced drugs, such as heroin and marijuana, which enter the United States directly from Mexico. Increasingly, cocaine is being moved into the United States by illegal aliens.

In its *International Narcotics Control Strategy Report*, issued in March 1991, the State Department's Bureau of International Narcotics Matters revealed:

> Mexico continues to produce about one-third of the heroin and 70 percent of the marijuana imported into the U.S. The [United States Government] estimates that over half the cocaine which entered the U.S. in 1990 transitted Mexico.[1]

The most alarming fact in the State Department's report is that "over half the cocaine which entered the U.S. in 1990 transitted Mexico." It reflected an increase of nearly 60 percent in the amount of cocaine coming into the United States from Mexico the year before. This, despite considerable progress in combatting the narcotics traffic reported in the same State Department document. Why?

Perhaps part of the answer, at least, was supplied by then INS Commissioner Alan Nelson in testimony he gave to Congress back in 1986, wherein he reported:

Commercial drug smuggling operations across the land border, and between the ports of entry, primarily utilize aliens to actually introduce the narcotics into the United States.[2]

Appearing before the House Subcommittee on Crime on May 22, 1986, Nelson stressed the interaction of illegal immigration and drug trafficking. As a major example, he reported that of 1,600 arrests made by the Los Angeles Police in anti-narcotic operations the previous year, 63 percent were illegal aliens.

Organized drug rings are using illegal immigrants to carry drugs into the United States more frequently. There is also substantial evidence that drug dealers and drug rings operating inside the United States seek out illegal immigrants already here and recruit them for their operations in this country. Though the number of illegal immigrants involved in drug trafficking constitute a small minority of all illegal aliens, they represent a significant problem nonetheless.

The reasons are: 1) the huge volume of narcotics brought into the United States by illegal aliens across the Mexico-U.S. border; 2) the ease with which narcotraficantes can cross the border without detection, and 3) the vulnerability of illegal immigrants once they are inside this country, particularly the unskilled and the less educated, who are likely to be easy victims of drug dealers because of their insecure status. The traffickers themselves are often from the same country as the illegal aliens — usually Mexico — and can offer them monetary rewards beyond their wildest dreams.

Up to $200 a trip appears to be the going rate for armies of poverty-stricken Mexicans in small border towns, to wade across the Río Grande with 100-pound loads of marijuana on their backs, according to a news account in the *Washington Post*.[3] These are inveterate illegals who bypass entry ports every day, leave their payload in "stash houses" on the U.S. side, then return home.

In testimony before the Western Hemisphere Affairs Subcommittee of the Senate Foreign Relations Committee on May 13, 1986, William von Raab, then Commissioner of the U.S. Customs Service, declared that "our Southwest border has become a serious problem of crisis proportions with respect to the trafficking of narcotics across it."[4] The Commissioner added that not only did the problem involve a lack of enforcement of U.S. immigration laws, but also was aggravated by the chronic corruption of Mexican law enforcement officials. Von Raab stated:

> As long as drug smugglers are free either to return their planes to Mexico and land in a safe haven, or, for that matter, penny ante drug smugglers are free just to quickly rush across the Río Grande River and find themselves their own safe haven, the United States effort is doomed to failure. There is no way that we can put a line of men and women across a 2,000 mile border as long as drug smugglers would be free to move right back into Mexico and not be prosecuted, or even cared about in this effort.[5]

Von Raab also indicated to the Senate Subcommittee that both Colombian and Cuban narcotics traffickers had moved into the Río Grande Valley, as a result of pressures from law enforcement authorities in Florida and California.

As the U.S. drug interdiction program has become more effective in recent years, in Florida and along our Gulf and East Coasts (with the use of aircraft and ships belonging to various U.S. Government agencies), drug producers, cartels, and smugglers from Colombia and other South and Central American countries have found it much easier and safer to smuggle drugs into Mexico, then sneak them across the porous Mexico-U.S. border.

"It's easier to get the dope in here," the *Washington Post* story cited above quotes Horace Cavit of the El Paso Intelligence Center. "Police are running all over each other in Florida and the Mexican border has been ignored. It's 2,000 miles long and there are a million places you can cross."[6] The Intelligence Center was set up by several U.S. agencies to monitor the smuggling of narcotics, firearms, and aliens.

Needless to say, the drugs and the persons smuggling them enter the United States by avoiding any type of border inspection, thus violating both our Customs and Immigration laws (as well as, of course, our criminal drug laws). Though some narcotics arrive in light planes which land and take off at remote tiny airstrips, much of it comes in by land, either by smugglers on foot, or, increasingly, in cars.

Von Raab reported, further, that a dramatic increase had taken place in the amount of "black tar" heroin being smuggled in from Mexico and that the Drug Enforcement Administration (DEA) had found that illegal aliens and migrant workers were the major source of that substance.

Cocaine smuggling has been increasing at a very rapid rate since the Colombian drug cartels began to use Mexico as a trampoline. The DEA estimates that an average of three-quarters of a ton of cocaine a day is entering the United States through Brownsville, Texas, the *Washington Post* reported.[7] It noted that the drug is transported in all sorts of ways, hidden in produce, equipment, cattle trucks, or simply, on human bodies.

***

"Narcotics is one of the most important U.S.-Mexican bilateral issues, figuring most prominently in the meetings between President Salinas and President Bush and in other senior-level discussions," according to the 1991 U.S. *Narcotics Control Report*.[8]

By the same token, the degree of involvement of illegal immigration in drug trafficking across the border should receive an equal amount of attention from the highest levels of both governments. So far, however, there is no evidence of that.

The U.S. Government is completely persuaded, at least publicly, that its Mexican partner is thoroughly committed to the war on drugs. The *Narcotics Control Report* states that the "Permanent Campaign Against Drug Trafficking" of the Mexican Government

has produced concrete results. Mexican law enforcement officials report seizing over 48 metric tons of cocaine, 395 kgs of opiates (including 176 kgs of heroin), 408 metric tons of marijuana and made 18,194 drug-related arrests in 1990.[9]

Attesting to the gigantic proportions of the Mexican drug traffic, the narcotics-related assets seized under Salinas's Presidency, so far, "are in excess of $1 billion," reports the same document.

Among other Mexican accomplishments in the drug war listed by the *Narcotics Control Report* are these:

• Creation of a Northern Border Response Force, "a rapid response team of MFJP [Mexican Federal Judicial

Police] agents established to interdict airborne South American cocaine traffickers."

• Establishment in the U.S. Embassy of a Tactical Analysis Team (TAT) "to facilitate exchange of tactical intelligence with the GOM in support of the [Response Force]."

• Participation of Mexican law enforcement and military personnel in training programs offered by the U.S. Customs Service, Coast Guard, FBI, and Drug Enforcement Administration.

• Participation of U.S. personnel in eradication verification and reconnaissance flights carried out by the Mexican Attorney General's Office.

Given minor attention by the State Department document but among the most significant weaknesses in the Mexican anti-drug program is corruption. Its report acknowledges that, "[c]orruption has impeded the GOM's narcotics control effort," then adds quickly, "[r]ooting out corruption, particularly within the police and the military forces, is a major goal of President Salinas's administration."[10]

Salinas has indeed cracked down on Mexican narcotics criminals and on the narcotics traffic to a much greater degree than any of his predecessors. He has also taken energetic measures to reduce corruption among Mexican officials. Under his Presidency, some of Mexico's top leaders and druglords have been arrested and jailed on charges of corruption and drug trafficking. Among them are the once all-powerful leader of the oilworkers union, and the former head of the federal security police and several accomplices. "[A]ll but two of the [15] major drug traffickers in Mexico have been jailed," the State Department reports with satisfaction. Included are a pair of the very biggest leaders of the Mexican drug Mafia, Rafael Caro Quintero and Ernesto Fonseca Carrillo; each was sentenced to 40 years in prison for the brutal murders of DEA Agent Enrique Camarena and his Mexican pilot, Alfredo Zavala, in February 1985.

These admittedly notable achievements have not, however, damaged seriously the highly lucrative drug trade across the Mexican border, nor deterred illegal aliens from becoming involved in it whether involuntarily or not. The chilling prospect is that Mexico may be ridden with a "narcopolitical system" which thus far has resisted the strongest efforts by Salinas to curtail its power. "The Mexican Narcopolitical System" has been described in detail by Javier Livas, a Mexican analyst, in *Mexico-United States Report*, a newsletter published by the Mexico-United States Institute, and personalized in the book, *Druglord — the Life and Death of a Mexican Kingpin*, by El Paso journalist Terrence E. Poppa. Writes Livas:

> Drug smuggling is a growing business because the demand for drugs is on the rise. For the narcotraffickers, the chances of obtaining fabulous riches are so great that it becomes very easy, and very profitable, to corrupt or threaten police and government officials. In turn, police officers and government functionaries with a propensity toward corruption are extremely attracted, so it behooves them to make deals with the traffickers while at the same time trying to protect themselves. Their experience in police work, their familiarity with the law, and the impunity they enjoy enable them to operate with very little risk in another homeostat which is equally or even more stable than the first. It is a homeostat of corruption which generates a great deal of money.[11]

A homeostat, explains Livas, is a state of equilibrium that exists between two elements. The basic narcotrafficking system is composed of "two classic elements that establish a primary balance: supply and demand. There are no drugs without buyers, and no buyers without drugs." Thus both elements are in equilibrium.

> The homeostat of corruption is put together slowly. The first connection—this, a direct one—is established between Income and Bribery. The greater the income of the narcos, the more police bribery there is. The goal is to reduce police actions to a minimum. At the same time, Police Power, divorced from ethical considerations, increases directly through collecting bribes—*mordidas*.
>
> [But] one of the undesirable effects for the narcos of increased police protection is that it also increases the number of persons involved and intensifies the internal rivalries among diverse police forces. The involvement of the Federal Judicial Police, some agencies of the Department of Government [*Gobernación*]—such as the Directorate General of National Security—National Security agents, Army personnel, the judicial police on the state and local levels and even municipal commanders, is well known in Mexico.[12]

However, all this poses a two-fold risk to the system. Livas maintains that

> the number of people involved is directly proportionate to the information available to Police Power. This, in turn, enhances the illegal relationship that constitutes the Triangle of Ambition. Clearly, the Information Available considerably increases Police Power (and its extortion power as well). Police chiefs not only have the law and money on their side, they also have abundant information.[13]

To protect themselves against information leaks, all the parties concerned band themselves into a "mafia." They take oaths of silence backed up by implicit death threats. Poppa's druglord, Pablo Acosta, was killed by his police partners in the Mexican border town, Ojinaga, where he ran the *"plaza"*—the local narcotics monopoly—with police protection. The police killed him not to eliminate the racket but, rather, to protect it. As Poppa explains:

> Sometimes, the authorities would protect their man from his rivals; other times they wouldn't, preferring a variety of natural selection to determine who should run the plaza. If the plaza-holder got arrested or killed by the authorities, sometimes it was because he had stopped making his 'payments'—or his name had started to appear in the press too frequently. Sometimes international pressure was so strong that the Government had been forced to take action against a specific individual.[14]

It was a system that enabled some authorities to keep a lid on drugs and profit handsomely from it at the same time.

That was confirmed by Von Raab in his testimony before a Senate subcommittee, when he observed that "armed Mexican authorities have been crossing the border on a regular basis to provide security for drug operations."[15]

One of the most notorious cases of protection of drug traffickers by Mexican authorities is that of the former chief of the Federal Security Directorate, José Antonio Zorrilla, who was arrested in 1990. All the relevant facts in the case have yet to be brought to public light, particularly those which may implicate top officials who served during the same time as Zorilla.

Livas continues:

> Through payoffs to police, soldiers and public officials, the narcos can avoid arrest and obtain protection. But the payoffs inevitably create a trap for them. Police control over the Narcotraffic Homeostat increases in proportion to the increase in the resources and the information available to the police.
>
> As information is leaked to the public, the pressure on the Government grows. It is then that the police use the information they possess against the narcos. Every corrupt cop becomes the narco's mortal enemy and tries to silence his corruptor, certain that it is merely a question of time until someone else replaces the eliminated narco and renews the mordidas.[16]

A bloody drama enacted in the prison of Matamoros, a Mexican border town, in May 1991, seemed to provide uncanny confirmation of Livas and Poppa's thesis of the mafia-police interplay which sustains the Mexican drug traffic. A convicted druglord, Oliverio Chávez Araujo, was shot in the eye and mouth by a rival gang over control of "lucrative cocaine routes" from Colombia worth $100 million a year, according to an on-the-spot report by the *New York Times*'s Mexico bureau chief, Mark Uhlig.[17]

The rival druglord, Juan García Abrego, had been abducting Chávez's men from prison, then killing them and dumping their bodies in Brownsville, Texas, opposite Matamoros. Chávez, who had been conducting his narcotics business as usual from a lavish jail cell replete with FAX machine and cellular phones, retaliated by taking over the prison in a shootout on May 17 which cost 18 lives. He charged that a hitman had been paid to assassinate him and that Mexican Federal Judicial Police agents were implicated.

The charge was "in line with accusations by the local police and American drug-enforcement officials, who say corrupt Federal police officers played a role in the gang warfare that provoked the [Chávez] takeover [of the prison]," according to Uhlig. "American investigators," he added, "have considered those killings [of Chávez's men] to be Federal Judicial Police operations."[18] Mexico's Federal police were, in short, siding with one druglord against the other in order to protect their stake in the narcotics racket, exactly as Livas and Poppa had described.

The most revealing episode, however, took place not in Matamoros but in Mexico City, the nation's capital. Uhlig reported that President Salinas had fired the Attorney General of Mexico, Enrique Alvarez del Castillo, "in reaction to the crisis" arising from the prison shootout. It was the first time that the dismissal of Mexico's highest law enforcement official had been reported in the American media. Yet it was pregnant with meaning. For Alvarez del Castillo had served as Governor of Jalisco during the period when its capital and Mexico's second city, Guadalajara, came under the virtual dominance of the Mexican narcotics mafia. Such was its power that in broad daylight it could kidnap the U.S. Drug Enforcement Administration agent, Enrique Camarena, and finally torture and kill him under the noses of the government and police. In fact, evidence later showed that police officers actually carried out the grisly operation, under mafia orders and in collaboration with it.

It was information "leaks" in the Camarena case that finally compelled the Mexican authorities to jail at least two of the chiefs, Caro Quintero and Fonseca Carrillo, as it probably moved Salinas to fire his Attorney General during the Matamoros crisis. The Camarena "leaks" were intelligence gathered by the DEA from Mexican police sources and conveyed to the U.S. Government and journalists, ultimately creating an international uproar. The same scenario played out in the Matamoros incident. Uhlig's report in the *Times* had all the earmarks of an intelligence "leak," and put international pressure upon Salinas at a critical moment, only days before the U.S. Congress was to vote on extending the fast-track authority to negotiate a free trade pact Mexico sorely needed. That probably motivated him also to dismiss Federal Judicial Police commanders in Tamaulipas, where Matamoros is located. (If Caro Quintero and Fonseca Carrillo escaped the sanguinary fate of Pablo Acosta, it is because they did not break the oath of silence although they undoubtedly knew a great deal about corruption in Mexican police and political circles.)

Livas continues:

> The narcos find themselves in the plight of the sorcerer's apprentice. They have created a machine that is fed automatically by the insatiable ambition of the police and/or corrupt public officials, and there is no way of stopping it.

The more money the police exact from the narcos, the more vulnerable do they become. And if they refuse to pay further mordidas, the police inform on them. The narcos suddenly find themselves on a list of "attackables" or "extraditables."[19]

The grave danger, in Mexico's case, is that its economy could become transformed into a "narcoeconomy," like that of Colombia, concludes Livas.

As long as the drug traffic is shot through with bribery, its break-even point will go much higher and more drugs will be sold. When the economy of an entire nation is based on drug trafficking, as is happening in Colombia, it becomes a narcoeconomy. Contributions from the 'extraditables' to their needy countrymen raise the break-even point of narco-trafficking even higher.[20]

An insight into this possibility was provided, perhaps inadvertently, by the State Department's *Narcotics Control Report*, when it observed:

While Mexico is not considered a major money laundering center — it is neither a tax haven nor a banking center — drug traffickers reinvest drug proceeds in personal property, land, and business.[21]

That is exactly the path followed by their Colombian counterparts.

***

Drug-smuggling by illegal border crossers has contributed to a rising tide of automobile thefts and firearms violations in southwestern communities. During Congressional testimony he gave in 1989, Police Chief Peter Ronstadt of Tucson, Arizona, said the undefended border was contributing to a rising tide of violence in his community, most of it among Mexicans. He called for increased military patrols of the border. Ronstadt said 62 percent of the unrecovered vehicles stolen from the Tucson area had been taken to Mexico. He said that his information was that the vehicles "were being traded for drugs, sold for cash to buy drugs, or used to transport drugs."[22]

Michael Huckaby, agent of the Bureau of Alcohol, Tobacco and Firearms in Arizona, testified at the same hearings on the growth of illicit purchases and smuggling into Mexico of arms, in many instances involving illegal aliens (who are prohibited by Federal law from purchasing or owning weapons). In one case, in 1988, ATF was called in when U.S. Border Patrol agents in Texas captured an illegal alien in possession of 19 firearms, 8 of which were classified as machine guns. The weapons had been stolen in Houston, Texas, reported Huckaby.[23]

If drug smuggling across the border and the ancillary crimes and violence it encourages are apparently intractable, it should be less difficult to find some means of controlling, at least, the acts of the decided minority of illegal aliens who contribute to such crimes. For one thing, just as the INS posts signs on the Mexican side of the border warning that a cold and inhospitable desert awaits illegals on the U.S. side, perhaps they could be forewarned also that arrest and jail could be the lot of those who aid the traffickers in drugs, stolen cars, and firearms.

9

The Threat of Urban Racial and Ethnic Tension

ON SUNDAY EVENING, May 5, 1991, the quiet residential neighborhood of Mount Pleasant, in northwest Washington, D.C., erupted in violence. Hundreds of youths hurled rocks and bottles at police officers brought in to maintain order, and looted local restaurants, drugstores, a clothier, a dry-cleaning establishment, a bicycle shop. . . for a total of 31 businesses attacked. They set cars and trucks on fire, among them 20 police cars and two dozen Metro transit vehicles which were destroyed or seriously damaged. The rioting and looting continued through Monday evening when a curfew was imposed.

The curfew, ordered by Washington's Mayor Sharon Pratt Dixon, was maintained through the next day by 1,500 Metropolitan Police officers including many in riot gear who used tear gas. Tension finally subsided by 5 a. m., Wednesday, when the curfew was lifted. More than 200 persons had been arrested. Miraculously, few were injured and nobody was killed.

The rioting began when three Metropolitan Police officers stopped a 30-year-old Salvadoran immigrant who had been drinking in a park and appeared to be drunk. A Hispanic female officer cuffed one of his hands, and with the other he withdrew a knife and brandished it at her companion, a black female officer. The latter shot him in the chest, not fatally. Passersby claimed, however, that he had been shot while both hands were cuffed. Word of the incident spread

79

throughout Mount Pleasant like wildfire, and irate Hispanic youths went on a rampage.*

About 27 per cent of Mount Pleasant's 11,000 residents are Hispanics, mainly immigrants from El Salvador, Guatemala, and Nicaragua. Another 35 per cent are black and an equal proportion white. Once predominantly black, the neighborhood is becoming more and more Hispanic; according to the 1990 Census, Hispanics had increased by 129 per cent since 1980 and non-Hispanic whites by 16 per cent, while blacks decreased by 20 per cent.

Many of Mount Pleasant's Hispanic residents are illegal immigrants. Others had acquired legal status only in October 1990, when Congress passed a bill which suspends for 18 months deportation proceedings against Salvadorans who had entered the country illegally. Much the same pattern obtains throughout the District of Columbia, most of whose Latin residents are immigrants.

Police abuse was the immediate cause of the Mount Pleasant violence. Neighborhood Hispanics are virtually unanimous in accusing city police, nearly all of whom are black, of treating them unfairly. The district's representative on the D.C. City Council, Frank Smith, Jr., a black, frankly acknowledged:

> The Hispanics see the police department as an occupying force the same way black people saw the police department as an occupying force in '68.[1]

He alluded to the 1968 Washington race riot in the wake of the Rev. Martin Luther King, Jr's assassination. Local blacks laid waste to ten city blocks and shocked the white establishment into a realization that they had to be treated differently otherwise further violence would ensue.

A black woman who worked in a Mount Pleasant supermarket also recalled that period. "The Spanish people are going to have to be heard the way we were in 1968," she said. "They are in the streets with no hope."[2]

---

*To keep the record straight, on the second night of rioting, May 6, those who ran amok were predominantly black youngsters, most of them from outlying areas. However, the root of the violence was the dire living conditions of local Hispanics, and in particular, perceived discrimination by black police and black leaders in general.

A Hispanic resident of Mount Pleasant added:

> They're standing up for their rights. This explosion has been brewing in the community for a long time. If you live here, you see a lot of abuse by police.[3]

Central American immigrants made comparisons with the police in their own countries. One, a Guatemalan, observed:

> It's just like Guatemala, except that what happens back home during the day happens here at night. The people took reprisals for the Latino brother.[4]

The underlying problem was that Mount Pleasant's Hispanic immigrants had not become assimilated into the community. "They are people who don't understand the culture," as it was put by Pedro Luján, a Peruvian who owns a popular local bakery. "When Americans start talking at the level of some of these [community] groups, they do not understand. They just walk away."[5]

The Salvadoran man shot by the police was a case in point. He had been apprehended for drinking in public. He could not understand that, while public drinking is accepted in his homeland, it is prohibited in America. It often leads, in Mount Pleasant, to other unlawful acts, such as urinating in the street, throwing garbage on the sidewalk, harassing women and elderly people, and sometimes pulling knives out on each other — all of which non-Hispanic residents complained about.

The great majority of Hispanic immigrants in Mount Pleasant, and in the capital generally, have a limited education—few, for example, speak English reasonably well or at all; this automatically creates a problem in communicating with official agencies such as the police. They tend to work in unskilled, lower-paid jobs in construction, restaurants, and other service enterprises. (The Salvadoran shot by the police was a construction worker who had been living in Washington about two years.) To make matters worse, many of Mount Pleasant's Hispanics had been laid off since the recession began, and were unable to obtain new employment. Generally, they lived in near-slum conditions.

Mayor Dixon and other black leaders complained that Hispanics have not tried hard enough to integrate into the community. After the riot, she stated publicly:

> I do think that in order to become a part of the community here you have to make an effort. Hispanics are not involved in ANC [Advisory Neighborhood Councils] or town meetings. They say when in Rome do as the Romans do. . . .It's to everyone's advantage to learn how to speak English . . . . You cannot have people drinking in public, because that is an inappropriate and criminal activity.... And you have to respond to that symbol of authority in whatever form it takes in our culture. . . . [6]

A more extreme attitude was expressed by a black member of the D.C. City Council, H. R. Crawford, who exploded: "If they don't appreciate our country, get out."[7] Crawford's words were especially jarring to Hispanics because he headed the Council's Human Services Committee.

A 28-year resident of Mount Pleasant, Larry Fredette, addressed the assimilation issue head-on:

> The people of the neighborhood are tired of having to assimilate to the Hispanics. This is their adopted home. It's time for them to assimilate to the American way of life.[8]

On the other hand, Hispanic leaders pointed out that their community throughout the Washington area had generally exercised great restraint under increasingly adverse living conditions. Regardless of how or why they had reached the area, or what immigration status they occupied, they faced severe deprivation—bad housing, unemployment, undernourishment, and virtually ubiquitous discrimination—without complaining.

One Hispanic leader added that the Salvadorans, who form the big majority of Hispanics in Mount Pleasant and adjoining Adams Morgan and Columbia Heights, were hard-working and frugal. The failure of the Latin Investment Corporation in December had wiped out their savings, yet they did not break out in angry protest. "But they were stressed out," the leader explained. The shooting of one of their number was apparently the last straw.[9]

The suspicion that Central American politics might have been injected into the Hispanic protest seemed to arouse general concern.

Mayor Dixon flatly charged, on a CBS Sunday talk show exactly one week after the rioting, that the riot "had some dynamics of terrorism, given the nature of some of the firebombs placed in cars."[10]

Both the *New York Times* and the *Washington Post* carried stories that former leftist guerrillas from Central America played a role in the violence. The *Times* reported that the acronyms of three Marxist groups fighting the Salvadoran Government were scrawled on walls in Mount Pleasant. An unemployed Salvadoran it interviewed, said:

> The same oppression that there is in my country, there is here too. The police are the same as in El Salvador. For the simple pleasure of it, they harass people. The rioting is the response to years of oppression.[11]

Two Salvadoran youths interviewed by the *Post* had reached Washington by crossing the border illegally at Tijuana. Asked about the acronym, "FPL," which with like graffiti "have appeared up and down Mount Pleasant Street," they said it stood for Popular Liberation Forces, the largest of five guerrilla groups still fighting El Salvador's elected government. The reporter, Gabriel Escobar, continued:

> They said some of those who on Sunday and Monday attacked police officers—the focus of their enmity because of the shooting of a Salvadoran construction worker—were former FPL guerrillas. The signature left in red along Mount Pleasant showed their transplanted disdain for authority —the police and, by extension, the city government.[12]

Clearly, the two young Salvadoran illegals were trained to engender disdain for law and order among fellow nationals and other Hispanics. That this could have wider consequences was made clear by their subsequent remarks to Escobar. They told him that it was "lucky" that the rioters were not joined by Salvadorans from Northern Virginia who come from Chirilagua, a town in El Salvador, "implying that they would have been even more aggressive." The *Post* reporter added:

> Local Salvadorans say the town borders a region under rebel control, and some of those here have been exposed to battle or fled forced conscription.[13]

The irony of the Mount Pleasant violence was not lost on a black-ruled city which, only two decades earlier, had risen up against white domination. "After listening to the Hispanic young people I went home and told my wife it was like listening to myself 20 years ago,"[14] observed John Wilson, Chairman of the D.C. City Council, who at that time had been active in the Student Non-Violent Coordinating Committee.

Just as blacks were denied a share of power in Washington under white rule years ago, so Hispanics today are not welcomed by its black rulers. The capital's Hispanic population is estimated at about 10 per cent of the total, according to the Bureau of Census after factoring in an acknowledged undercount in its original figures, but holds less than 1 per cent of city government jobs. When the Mount Pleasant outbreak occurred there was not a single Hispanic on the City Council, or the School Board, and only two on the Advisory Neighborhood Councils.

The only high-level post available to the Hispanic community, the Office of Latino Affairs, remained unfilled (it was run by an interim director) from the date of Mayor Dixon's inaugural on January 2, 1991, through the riot and its aftermath. Washington's Hispanics had voted overwhelmingly for Dixon, an efficient, apparently upright former telephone company executive who represented a welcome change after years of Marion Barry's misgovernment. They expected Dixon to show some sensitivity to their problems, but when it came to naming a suitable person to head the Office of Latino Affairs, she chose instead to appoint a commission to make recommendations and then rejected the names of three Hispanics it proposed.

The fact is that the riot took Mayor Dixon and Washington's black establishment by surprise. If Dixon's unawareness may be attributed to lack of political experience and newness on the job, that could not be said of the city's black leadership as a whole. For that matter, neither did the national Hispanic or black leadership express much concern about the plight of local Hispanic residents or any inkling of oncoming trouble. The Rev. Jesse L. Jackson, who had been elected the District's "shadow senator" in November 1990, was not his usual vocal self on this issue. The founder of the "Rainbow Coalition," which he had organized to unite all minorities under a single umbrella, did not appear on the riot scene until the third day; showing up outside the community center where several hundred local youths were gathered, he told them to disperse and go home.

***

Washington had become the mirror image of Miami. Violent racial and other ethnic riots in the United States used to be directed primarily by blacks against whites, or vice versa—and on rare occasions by Hispanics and others against non-Hispanic whites. But in the 1980s, a new and disturbing trend manifested itself: Racial and ethnic animosity erupted into violence *directed by one minority against another*. The new trend was reflected in two major disturbances which occurred in Miami involving Hispanics and blacks.

In May 1980, the frustrated and largely economically deprived black community went on a rampage after 125,000 Cubans debarked from the port of Mariel, Cuba, among them a substantial number of criminals, wastrels, sex deviates, and other undesirables. The *marielitos* were allowed by Fidel Castro to leave Cuba freely, in the hope that they would prove indigestible to American society. They became a *casus belli* for blacks.

Underneath it all, the blacks were expressing their frustration and resentment at losing employment and business opportunities, as well as a chance to share political power, due to the overwhelming influx of Cuban refugees over the preceding two decades and their rise to economic and political dominance. When the Cubans were followed by large numbers of Nicaraguans, Colombians, and Dominicans, Miami became a Latin city and the blacks were virtually isolated. As Melvin Oliver and James H. Johnson, Jr., two black social scientists, describe the origins of the May 1980 riots:

> Competing for similar jobs in the unskilled and service sectors of the city's economy, blacks found themselves losing to Cubans at an alarming rate. Cuban faces soon replaced blacks in such competitive sectors of the economy as hotels, hospitals and restaurants. Employers claimed to find the Cubans more willing to take menial jobs for minimum and below minimum wages. Blacks felt an extreme sense of injustice in the way in which they were being passed, economically and socially, by the more recent Cuban arrivals.[15]

In 1988, another black-Hispanic outbreak occurred in Miami, when a Hispanic policemen of Colombian origin shot and killed a black youth who failed to halt when ordered. At the time, tensions between the black and Hispanic communities also appear to have built up in other parts of the country. In the Los Angeles metropolitan area, blacks in ghettoes such as Watts felt increasingly threatened with job losses and the loss or diminution of social and other benefits and opportunities, due to the unrelenting immigration of large numbers of legal and illegal immigrants from Mexico. According to Oliver and Johnson:

> Competition for housing [in Watts] has turned intense. Public services that blacks feel they fought hard to earn are being utilized in large numbers by Latino newcomers. For example, nearly three out of every four children born at Martin Luther King County Hospital are Latino. Heavy Latino use of these facilities is frowned on by some Blacks.... Latinos on the other hand do not feel welcome in these communities. Fear of violence and crime is an important factor.... While overt social conflict has not exploded, in the words of a close observer, 'it's a potential powder keg ... it's just a matter of time.'[16]

Each year now brings nearly a million legal and illegal immigrants to the United States, Frank Morris, another black scholar, told the House Subcommittee on Immigration on March 13, 1990. Forty to forty-five percent of them — illegals, in the great majority — will settle in New York, Los Angeles, Miami, Chicago, Houston and San Francisco-Oakland, he calculated. Some 6 million black Americans, about one-fifth of the nation's black population, currently live and work in those metropolitan areas. Millions of other black Americans would consider migrating to them, holds Morris, if job prospects were not dimmed by the foreign newcomers.[17]

Morris estimated that many of the illegal aliens, lacking skills and training, will be forced to seek jobs in occupations where black Americans are already overrepresented: building services and maintenance, construction, light manufacturing, non-professional health care, hotels and restaurants. Wages and working conditions will be adversely affected.

Similarly, blacks resent the high price they pay in terms of quality public education for their children in major cities of illegal immigrant settlement, such as Los Angeles and Houston. Their inner cities are settled with families whose children, Morris testified, require special help for limited English proficiency.

Heavy immigration may be affecting the mobility of black workers and altering migration patterns with the United States, believes Professor Vernon Briggs of Cornell University, writing in the *New York Times*. The rate of black migration to Los Angeles and other major California urban centers has slowed markedly in the past two decades. Briggs found that a major factor in the rising percentage of blacks resettling in the South since the 1960s is the resumption of mass immigration from Latin America and Asia into Eastern, Midwestern, and Western cities.

Briggs's fears are echoed by another black analyst, Juan Williams, who is a reporter and columnist for the *Washington Post*. Exactly one week after the Mount Pleasant rioting began, Williams wrote in his newspaper:

> There could well be more such confrontations ahead in American cities as the Hispanic population grows. By the end of this decade, there will be more young Hispanics in the country than young blacks.[18]

***

Hispanic-black relations were further taxed by the Mount Pleasant outbreak. The loose coalition between the two minorities on broader civil rights issues had already suffered some strain. Initial black refusal to support the Hispanic position that employer sanctions against illegal aliens violate civil rights almost led to the breakup, in 1990, of the Leadership Coalition of minority civil rights activists.

Raúl Yzaguirre, President of the influential National Council of La Raza, pointed up the problem in a formal statement he made before its annual dinner on May 8, 1990. Recalling the vicissitudes of Hispanics in the United States, he complained that "our patience was confused with acquiescence, our manners were interpreted as timidity, our commitment to family was taken as evidence of lack of individuality, our tolerance was confused for resigned fatalism . . . ." He added pointedly:

Much of that history was repeated within the Leadership Conference on Civil Rights. Back in 1963, I became the first Hispanic member of this great coalition. For much of that period, we have experienced the pain of being an afterthought. We have watched as our issues were ignored. And we have witnessed a process that says to us that we do not count as much as other groups.

On two other occasions we have gone to the brink of parting company with the Leadership Conference. Up until two hours ago, we thought that we had to cross that brink.

We are persuaded that, as a result of our actions, this coalition has been permanently changed. That its member organizations will simply not tolerate massive levels of Government-sponsored discrimination to occur. The evidence is too clear, the harm is too pervasive.[19]

Yzaguirre added, in what seemed to be a veiled warning:

We will continue to have hope in the civil rights community, but know that our hope is not unlimited, that our patience can not be taken for granted, and that our faith is not fathomless.[20]

Although the National Association for the Advancement of Colored People subsequently approved an anti-employer sanctions resolution to mollify Hispanics, some local NAACP leaders continue to speak out in support of sanctions to protect the job opportunities of black Americans, reported the *New York Times* on October 5, 1990.

The conflict may become more acute over the issues of political representation and access to affirmative action benefits in immigrant-impacted states like California. Linda Chávez, former head of the White House Office of Public Liaison, dwelt on that possibility in a piece for the *New Republic* entitled "Rainbow Collision — the Hispanic-Black Feud," a derisive allusion to Jesse Jackson's much publicized Rainbow Coalition. She wrote:

What blacks — and whites — are finding more difficult to accept is that many Hispanics are clearly willing to build political influence through gerrymandering districts composed largely of non-U.S. citizens, many of whom are illegal. At a recent conference on the voting rights act, the former president of MALDEF [Mexican American Legal Defense Fund], Joaquin Avila, suggested that non-citizens be allowed to vote — a proposal even most Hispanic leaders are wary of endorsing. Illegal aliens are already included in census counts used to reapportion legislative districts, a policy that was upheld in a 1989 Supreme Court ruling. Some Hispanic districts consist of only half the number of eligible voters as non-Hispanic districts, which gives voters twice the voting power of those in other districts.[21]

The Los Angeles County Office of Affirmative Action found, in 1988, that while Hispanics were 27.6 percent of the County's population (according to the 1980 census), they were only 18.3 percent of its workforce. It found that blacks were only 12.6 percent of the population, but 30.5 percent of the county work force. Those percentages have changed very little since then. The Office recommended aggressive recruiting of Hispanics over five years to bring about "population parity," and the County Board of Supervisors agreed. Black leaders noted that the black jobholders, who tend to fill the county's lower wage jobs, are likely to suffer. The Black Employees Association complained that the figures used to calculate Hispanic parity are inflated by large numbers of illegal aliens, reported Peter Skerry, an authority on Hispanic affairs, in 1989.

Demographic shifts in Los Angeles, sparked by illegal immigration, are eclipsing black political power there. Blacks' share of the city population has slipped from 18 percent to 12 percent in two decades, a trend confirmed by the 1990 census, which records a 3.3 per cent drop in black inhabitants over the past decade. In the same period, Hispanics increased their number by an extraordinary 70.7 per cent. Many observers expect Tom Bradley will be the last black mayor of Los Angeles and that black representation on the City Council will decline. One black political leader said the Mexicans came in riding on "black coattails," and in the 1990s they will control the school district and there will be a Latino mayor. "Blacks," predicted Joel Klotkin in the *Washington Post*, "will lose in the shuffle."[22]

Although the potential for conflict appears greatest between black Americans and Hispanic immigrants, mainly the illegals, other recent immigrant groups also seem to be the objects of resentment and protest actions. These could, if not defused, lead to violence and other negative consequences that are costly for the nation: isolation, bitterness, vindictive politics. Unhappily, resultant severe tensions have taken their toll in New York, where in 1990 blacks repeatedly called boycotts and protest actions against immigrant Korean grocers in black areas of the city. They indicate that the Asian community, whose members are increasing at a rate only second to that of Hispanics, is not immune to the racial conflict that already exists between Hispanics and blacks in America's urban areas.

10

Separatism or Assimilation

IS THERE A DANGER that the presence of ever-growing numbers of immigrants of Mexican origin, particularly illegals, will lead to cultural and, eventually, political separatism? Is it possible that some day separatism will become secessionism, and a Hispanic "Quebec" will emerge to challenge the Union with its own declaration of independence? Some U.S. scholars and journalists have voiced such fears, as have also some Mexican-Americans. Does separatism, or irredentism, find serious support within the Mexican-American community?

There is no evidence that mainstream Mexican-Americans have the slightest interest in any form of separatism; on the contrary, their energies and minds appear directed toward becoming assimilated into American society and in that endeavor they have achieved remarkable success. A tiny, vociferous minority of extremists does advocate separatism, but it is taken seriously only by a few commentators with little first-hand knowledge of Mexican-Americans.

Some U.S. analysts view the concentration of masses of people of Mexican origin in the Southwest as making for "divisiveness," as it is put by Georges Fauriol, Director for Latin American Studies of the Center for Strategic and International Studies in Washington. He sees current immigration trends as virtually threatening America's unity in the future:

> There is concern that the growing use of racial or ethnopolitical power blocs in the U.S. will foster a divisiveness within American society. The issue is not stated here lightly. Since the 1970s, for example, bilingualism

91

92

has become a highly visible public agenda in school, governments, and media. Its relationship with present trends of large migration flows of people of Spanish-speaking countries is obvious. Ethnic power group manipulation of U.S. foreign policy is nothing new. Will a nation divided along ethnic lines be a united nation, able to carry on a bipartisan and consistent foreign policy?[1]

Fauriol's concerns are understandable, but the growth of "racial or ethnic political power blocs" in the United States is hardly new, as we know from the proliferation of Irish political machines in big cities in the past, or injurious: The election of a President of Irish ancestry did not exactly split America apart at the seams. As for "bilingualism," that is not a divisive *national* issue. Its meaning is debatable and it generates emotion in some quarters; but as long as rational discussion prevails, there is no reason why a happy medium cannot be reached. What offers real cause for worry is the unceasing influx of *illegal* immigrants, though the bogey of "a nation divided along ethnic lines" is not quite discernible on the horizon.

However, a U.S. commentator, William A. Henry III, who wrote a piece for *Time* magazine cited by Fauriol, believes the contrary:

The disruptive potential of bilingualism and biculturalism is worrisome: millions of voters cut off from the main sources of information, millions of would-be employees ill at ease in the language of their workmates.[2]

How removed from reality are Henry's concerns about such a searing emotional conflict as "dual ethnic loyalties" was, of course, dramatically underscored by the performance of U.S. soldiers of many ethnic backgrounds in the 1991 Persian Gulf war. During the long months of boredom and fear while their fates were being decided by others, and especially during the actual hostilities when life hung in the balance every moment, not a single untoward incident occurred among our multi-ethnic force of half a million men and women to so much as hint at a loyalty problem. Historically, in fact, our two biggest minorities, blacks and Hispanics, have been consistently distinguished in war for their bravery and unqualified dedication to country.

To be sure, there is deep discontent among Hispanics at their perceived isolation from the dominant Anglo society. Although most of the spurious legal, moral, and cultural bases for discrimination and segregation were swept away in the civil rights revolution of the 1960s —which also obtained for Hispanics their inclusion in programs of affirmative action and Spanish language voting rights—all too many persons of Latin American descent still experience discrimination. The main difference between then and now is that the civil rights revolution has given them a practical instrument to defend their rights and prosecute whoever may attempt to abridge them.

That the battle for those rights still continues, scarcely abated, is borne out repeatedly by one incident or another. The 1980s ended with a landmark court decision which drove home that point, when the U.S. District Court in El Paso decided in favor of 310 predominantly Mexican-American FBI agents who had brought a class-action suit charging the Bureau with discriminating against them. Though they won the suit, the fight goes on, only it has shifted to the field itself, where a Hispanic agent must still "prove" every day that he is worthy of a raise, a promotion, a transfer, but with this key difference: The FBI must follow court guidelines which prohibit it from pursuing the old practices.

Ethnic discrimination is perhaps the most basic of all factors militating against assimilation. The settlement of Europeans in the United States did not encounter a great deal of ethnic prejudice; Jews and Catholics were long objects of hatred and scorn (and still are largely), but essentially for religious, not racial reasons. The persistent racial and ethnic discrimination that Hispanics suffer in this country is second in degree and intensity only to that of the blacks, and goes back in time almost as far. Hispanics stand out, even when their English is flawless and their education excellent, simply because they are darker-skinned on the whole. Some are "Indian-looking," with square features and a vestige of the Oriental epicanthic fold in their eyes betraying probable Asian ancestry. Race, then, is the basis for much anti-Hispanic sentiment.

Younger Mexican-Americans are especially sensitive to any act or word that is perceived as a slight because of their ethnic make-up, for another revolution—that of rising expectations—has inculcated in them a strong sense of social values and personal worth. For that reason, they tend to react with outrage to stories they have heard of the crass prejudice suffered by their parents and grandparents. Also, they tend to belligerence against the "dominant society," and to impatience with slow-moving reforms. In consequence, some of them join street gangs to express their hatred and resentment, while others dream of their "own" society: not necessarily one that resurrects a mythical Mexico of old, nor yet an America "Mexican style." Ysidro Ramón Macías, writing on "The Chicano Movement," internalizes how some members of his generation feel:

> The Chicano is becoming more isolated from Anglo society than ever before because of the Anglo's refusal to accept him. The Chicano asks himself: 'Why should I try to prove myself to the Anglos? I will be my own man, respecting my heritage.'[3]

At various times in the past, extremists have tried to sow separatist ideas among Mexican-Americans, particularly the youth, but they have always been a tiny minority. Though vociferous, they are not heard. Their goals are, in any case, vague and shifting, with one exception: those who favor secession and the creation of a "Chicano Republic" or reunification with Mexico.

One small group called the *Movimento de Liberación Nacional* (MLN) has existed in the Southwest since 1977, agitating on both sides of the border to recover what it calls the "occupied territory torn from Mexico as a result of the U.S. invasion" a century and a half ago. The MLN claims that since the Treaty of Guadalupe-Hidalgo, in 1848, Mexicans "have been denied access to their resources, freedom of movement, protection under the law, the retention of their land and the right to self-determination in the occupied territory north of the Rio Grande," reports R. E. Butler.[4]

Some Anglo writers seem to accept at face value the propaganda of Chicano extremists that Mexican-Americans are up in arms over the "injustices" of the Guadalupe-Hidalgo Treaty. It is questionable, to begin with, that many Mexican-Americans are conversant with the Treaty. In any case, how many of them really worry about the territory Mexico lost a century and a half ago? The virtual disappearance from the scene of Chicano extremist groups seems proof enough that their message has fallen on deaf ears.

Much has been made of the supposed attachment of Mexicans and Mexican-Americans to the legendary land of the Aztecs called Aztlán, and the yearning to recreate it in the Southwest. But the myth lends itself more to poetry, and to leftist tracts, than to rational belief.* Some extremists have attempted to use the myth to promote Chicano irredentism, as in the 1969 "Spiritual Plan of Aztlan," which exhorts:

> We, the Chicano inhabitants and civilizers of the northern land of Aztlan, from whence came our forefathers, reclaiming the land of their birth and consecrating the determination of our people of the sun, declare that the call of our blood is our power, our responsibility, and our inevitable destiny . . . . With our heart in our hand and our hand in the soil we declare the independence of our *mestizo* nation.[5]

Anglo leftwing groups have also attempted to exploit what they imagine to be the Chicano's yearning for Aztlán. The Trotskyite Socialist Workers Party published an article in its organ, *The Militant*, by one Roberto González, which sought to identify Chicanos with Puerto Rican and black "liberation movements." González asserted:

> We have to start to consider ourselves as a nation. We can create a congress or *concilio*. We can understand that we are a nation of Aztlan. We can understand and identify with Puerto Rican liberation. We can understand and identify with Black liberation. We can understand and identify with white liberation from this oppressing system once we organize around ourselves.[6]

But such appeals have made no headway among Mexican-Americans. It is surprising, in fact, that causes embraced by the left have found a less sympathetic echo among that group than all but any other in American society. No call for a "Chicano Republic" has ever aroused, among Chicanos, anything resembling the fervor that the Communists' espousal of a separate "Black Republic" once did among blacks.

---

* The writer lived and worked in Mexico nearly a quarter of a century, and visited the border many times, without ever encountering a single serious discussion of Aztlán. I know of no serious Mexican scholar or journalist who professes to believe in it. Aztlán, I have concluded, exists largely in the minds of romantic U.S. writers and a handful of Chicano irredentists. Thinking Mexicans seem to concur.

All the more surprising is it to find that a respected Mexican immigration scholar, Arthur Corwin, seems to have contracted a bad case of "Aztlanitis." He avers:

> Perceptive writers no longer ignore the emergence of Mexico-America. This phenomenon has also been labeled 'Aztlán,' 'La Raza Unida,' 'The Other Mexico,' 'A Nation Within a Nation,' 'The Browning of America,' 'La Reconquista,' 'MexAmerica,' 'Chicano Quebec,' 'The Aztec Curse,' and 'Santa Anna's Revenge.' Whatever the label, Mexico-America is a dynamic, hybrid culture that manifests a symbiotic love-hate relationship between two vastly dissimilar cultures.
>
> As an ethnic conscience, it now spreads over the border states and has vigorous transplants all the way to the Latin barrio of Washington, D. C. It has already changed the course of Mexican acculturation and U.S.-Mexico relations. By 1990 it may embrace 30 million Raza folk. As never before, this Spanish-language soul culture has a flourishing network of educational and indoctrination programs. . . . It is very much a political subculture wherein Third Worldism and Raza brotherhood are the dominant ideologies. . . . Many patrons of ethnic programs see the social marginality and the racial complex of the Raza mentality as basically an American assimilation failure. . . . Perhaps the Raza migration and acculturation experience might be understood as a continuous transfer of the Indo-Mexican's race-conscious struggle, passive or active, against the white man's conquest institutions, whether semifeudal there or corporate here. In any case, Anglo-Americans and other ethnic Americans will have to learn either to live with the imported 'reconquista' mentality or to manipulate it.[7]

Corwin has confused two quite different concepts.

What he calls "Mexico-America" or "The Other Nation" is the intermingling that has been going on around the border for generations, as both Mexicans and Anglos work, trade, live, and socialize with each other more and more in the course of their daily lives. It is not a *conscious* striving to create a "another nation" but, rather, a natural process of cultural interpenetration that has given the border a special flavor — even, a uniqueness. Though people on both sides of it share many attitudes in common, including even a sense of independence from their respective central governments, the idea of creating a "new nation" seems unthinkable to them.

Yet Corwin appears to regard the special cultural mix along the border as separatist. He equates the natural "Mexico-America" process there with the deliberate intent of a few to create a "Chicano Quebec" or an "Aztlán," though the process is a reality while the latter is a myth. Corwin has also got his symbols mixed: "Mexico-America" is not *La Reconquista* — the "reconquest" of the territory Mexico lost in the 1848 war that some Mexicans living in the past may dream of. It is doubtful whether any thinking citizen of Ciudad Juárez dreams of "reconquering" El Paso, just opposite, when he finds it far more satisfying simply to enjoy its well-stocked stores, good restaurants, and clean streets. If anything, he would prefer to move to El Paso if he could, not take it over.

Indeed, the feeling one often encounters on the Mexican side of the border is a desire—which may be unstated but is apparent—*to be annexed by*, not to annex, the other side. That is often expressed, half in jest, by talk in Baja California, Chihuahua, Coahuila, or Tamaulipas of wanting to become the "51st state" of the American Union. Sometimes that feeling is articulated more formally, and in earnest, as when a poll taken in the Spring of 1991, at the height of the free-trade debate, found that 58 percent of Mexican respondents favored "economic integration" with the United States. Provided that integration—the same respondents would probably have added (had they been asked) would not cost them their Mexican identity.

To speak of "a political subculture wherein Third Worldism and Raza brotherhood are the dominant ideologies" is sheer hyperbole. This leads, not surprisingly, to Corwin's rash prediction that, by 1990, Mexico-America "may embrace 30 million Raza folk," as he stated in 1978, in his *Immigrants—and Immigrants: Perspectives of Mexican Labor Migration to the United States*, from which the long quotation cited above was taken. The 1990 Census has so far found a total of only 20.4 million persons of Hispanic origin in the entire United States, of which perhaps some 14 million are of Mexican descent. (Because they are undercounted, the real total of Hispanics is estimated to be nearly 22.4 million.) Even if all of them favored a "Mexico-America," which is hardly possible, that would be less than half of Corwin's predicted number.

***

Separatist notions have not thrived in the Mexican-American community, so far, simply because they offered no real solution to its problems. Its members would much rather make their way within the present system, and the idea of trying to set up another one, whether inside or outside of it — a Hispanic "Quebec," for example — does not appeal to them. The average Mexican-American citizen has become assimilated into the general culture and regards himself as American just like everyone else; some will point with pride, as a matter of fact, to their longer residence in this country than nearly the entire Anglo population. The younger generation, despite its restlessness, is imbued with the American spirit and culture and speaks English rather than Spanish. Try to speak Spanish to a Mexican-American, even one of the older generation, and he will probably feel embarrassed at his lack of fluency in the "mother tongue." English is the common language in the average Mexican-American citizen's home.

Even Mexican immigrants eventually use English as their primary language. Only 40 percent of them acquire a working knowledge of English in the beginning, according to K. F. McCarthy and R. B. Valdez.[8] RAND demographic researchers Georges Vernez and David Ronfeldt, who extrapolated from the McCarthy-Valdez study using 1980 Census figures in an article for *Science* magazine, add:

> By the second generation, there is a dramatic improvement in high school completion and in English proficiency. Nearly 90 percent have a working knowledge of English and only a residual 4 percent remain monolingual in Spanish.[9]

To be sure, Mexican-Americans proudly retain their own distinct traditions, language, and culture to the extent possible, and why not? In this respect, they follow the pattern of other immigrants and minorities — whether Germans, Italians, Jews, Poles, or Scandinavians — all of whom have preserved certain cultural and religious traditions of their motherlands while being unmistakably American. Indeed, when so-called hyphenated Americans go abroad they are never taken for anything else but Americans.

Mainline Hispanic leaders and organizations discount separatism as a threat, notwithstanding the huge numbers of illegal immigrants from Mexico (and Central America). They point to the record of the United States over the past century and a half in easily absorbing and assimilating millions of immigrants from countries in Europe and Asia, many from societies far different from the prevailing Anglo-American culture. They point out that the vast majority of those immigrants were readily assimilated into U.S. society, their children soon learned the English language and American customs, and within a relatively short period of time became part of the American "melting pot."

Indeed, the programs of such major Hispanic organizations as the League of United Latin American Citizens, by far the largest of them, stress working within the system. LULAC's jobs program, SER (an acronym which in Spanish means, "to be"), trains young Hispanics for executive and professional careers with the cooperation of big Anglo companies. The National Council of La Raza, once a radical group which advocated a kind of Hispanic-First philosophy bordering on separatism, has an impressive networking operation which involves both local Hispanic groups and leading Anglo corporations in a host of local development projects including jobs programs for unemployed Hispanics. On the political level, the Southwest Voters Registration Project has for years conducted an uphill, but gradually successful year-round campaign to get Hispanics to register to vote in local, state, and national elections.

On the other hand, LULAC, NCLR, and other Hispanic groups have opposed effective immigration controls and seem disinclined to entertain the very idea of them. They frown, for example, upon some sort of viable ID that would help screen illegal from legal immigrants without providing a pretext for police abuse.

Notwithstanding the generally pro-assimilation attitudes of mainline Hispanic organizations, certain factors militate against the assimilatory process and they must be addressed, for they impede the process and could generate separatist feeling. These factors, especially if they become progressively pronounced, could halt altogether, or could at least seriously delay, assimilation in areas of very high Mexican population density.

The evidence shows that the rate of assimilation among Mexican immigrants is slower than that of immigrants from Europe, and even Asia. The General Accounting Office found in a 1988 study that even Mexicans who arrive legally do not match the record of other immigrant groups in ultimately accepting U.S. citizenship. Mexicans have one of the lowest rates of naturalization, with only 18 percent of eligible aliens taking out U.S. citizenship, in contrast to much higher rates by other ethnic groups such as Cubans, Koreans, or Filipinos.[10]

One of the main factors that hinder the assimilatory process is the large volume and ceaseless flow of Mexican immigration, both legal and illegal. The big surge in European immigration at the turn of the century peaked during World War I. For half a century afterward, immigration from Europe was kept low, allowing a pause for the assimilation of the millions that had come between 1880 and 1910. No such "time-out" to enable the slow process of assimilation of Hispanics to mature has happened over the past generation, and seems unlikely to during the remainder of the century. With Mexico's working-age population growing at three percent annually, there is little prospect that the influx will abate in the foreseeable future. Dating from about 1965, then, the unceasing flow of Mexican immigrants has simply not permitted them enough time to assimilate.

As a result, in places like the Río Grande Valley of Texas and the *barrios* of Los Angeles, there are entire communities where a settler from Mexico has no need or incentive to learn English, and where he can function satisfactorily for the rest of his life speaking only Spanish, as Gerda Bikales and Gary Imhof found in their 1988 study.[11] In their public schools—the levelling institution where immigrants have traditionally mastered English—Mexican and Central American immigrant children may find themselves in a bilingual education program where they are taught all subjects in Spanish. Conceivably, those children will speak and learn exclusively in Spanish during their entire academic life, emerging in society deficient in the English language. (The original objective of the bilingual education program as mandated by the courts was, of course, to serve only as a transition mechanism to help children whose primary language is a foreign one to learn English.)

As long as Mexican immigrants cluster in U.S. cities already thickly populated by their predecessors, the chances of their assimilating into the general society progressively lessen: Why struggle to master a strange tongue if none of your neighbors uses it? Conversely, in such a narrowing, inward-looking environment, separatist notions could develop. On the other hand, how can the movement of immigrants into populous Hispanic-American communities be diverted to other areas with fewer Hispanics?

If it is argued that our previous experience demonstrates that new immigrants will, sooner or later, learn to speak English and practise the American way of life, that experience may not necessarily apply to the recent Mexican arrivals. This is due to a unique geographical phenomenon: *their homeland is contiguous with the United States*. All other nationalities which have settled in America came from distant lands and were effectively cut off from them once they settled in the New World. Eventually, contact with the old country was reduced to occasional visits, letters, exchanges of gifts, birthday greetings, and sometimes, marriages to a compatriot. These new settlers and their progeny had no other alternative than to adapt as rapidly as possible to their new country. That, however, is not the case with Mexican immigrants. Since their native land abuts the United States, they can go back and forth at will. In a sense, they never really leave home, for not only is it physically at hand but family members and friends continue to live there, or come to visit or live with them in the United States, and thus form an inextricable bond between immigrant and homeland. This is especially true, of course, of the border areas where intermingling is continuous.

Two groups of Mexican immigrants seem to resist the assimilation process most. One involves the 2.5 million former illegals of Mexican origin who were amnestied under IRCA. The second, and perhaps more indigestible group consists of the illegals who have settled in the United States since then and those who keep arriving here daily.

Speaking of the first group, Vernez and Ronfeldt concluded that

the sheer size of the newly legalized population will affect not only the speed and nature of their assimilation but that of their children, of other immigrant groups, and of future immigrants. Their economic progress will have a major effect on the nation's economic future. . . .[12]

The National Council of La Raza made a study of the results of the 1986 Immigration Reform and Control Act which provided valuable detail on what has happened to the 2.5 million Mexican immigrants who were legalized under it. The study noted that the success of the second stage, which still goes on, "depends upon the capacity of the nation's educational system to provide English as a Second Language (ESL) and civics courses to applicants who need them in order to fulfill requirements for permanent residence." Its conclusion:

> NCLR estimates that over 975,000 newly legalized persons nation-wide will need to enroll in ESL/civics classes in order to meet second-stage requirements.[13]

If nearly 30 percent of those legalized since 1986 still require English as a second language, one can readily imagine, first, how much longer it will take persons in that category to learn English as their primary tongue, and second, the length of time they will need to become fully assimilated. The realistic answer is probably that they will never assimilate, in view of the finding that no "time-out" for the assimilation process to mature is in prospect if, in the coming decades, immigration from Mexico continues apace.

The biggest impediment to assimilation is the illegal immigrant. His status is an insurmountable barrier to the initial steps that must be taken to become a U.S. citizen.

The high growth in illegal immigration from Mexico retards further the relatively slow rate of assimilation of the Mexican-American community in general. This could also contribute, unwittingly, to the germination of separatist ideas. Since they cannot legally become eligible for membership in the general society, or even in the mainstream Mexican-American community, the illegals confine themselves to existing enclaves which are already outside normal society, and that makes for separateness if not separatism.

Furthermore, the illegals differ from earlier waves of immigrants in important substantive ways, such as their generally lower educational level and low skills or absence of them, as Borjas has pointed out.

Nevertheless, the NCLR study of IRCA advocates a "second legalization program" for those who were illegals one year after the Act was passed. It states:

> Congress must . . . consider mechanisms for adjusting the status of undocumented residents of the U.S. by a means more effective than the recent legalization program. Such means could include a program which legalizes individuals living within the U.S. when IRCA was passed, or a second legalization program with a cutoff date that falls within one year of enactment.[14]

Legalizing more illegals will hardly contribute to resolving or even alleviating the basic problem of how to stem the flow of those who cross the border daily. Nor does it address the more vexing problem that follows illegal migration: How to enable the assimilatory process to absorb new millions of immigrants when there is no "time-out," no interregnum? Above all, the legalization of successive waves of illegal immigrants would amount to a *rolling amnesty*, as it were; it would represent an open invitation to endless millions of persons to cross the border at will, in the secure knowledge that eventually America would legalize their status. Obviously, this would vastly expand the indigestible mass of illegals in our midst and ultimately lead to an untenable situation.

Finally, if the crisis in Mexico continues and especially if economic conditions worsen, that will drive additional millions of Mexicans into the United States illegally, and intensify the twin problems of high population concentration and low assimilation rate. It is not impossible that among the new arrivals will arise forces which demand radical solutions to their plight, and enlist in their cause the illegal alien underclass and even legal Mexican residents and perhaps some Mexican-American citizens. Caught between economic failure in Mexico and inability to make headway in the United States, frustrated illegals might resort to confrontational tactics and even violence to obtain redress. Since they constitute an underclass already outside the law, what would they have to lose? The U.S. authorities could continue, of course, to deport them; but that cannot go on indefinitely and will not reduce the number of illegals entering this country. Illegal aliens could, then, eventually become a hotbed of agitation and disaffection which might at some point challenge the harmony and unity of American society.

11

A Potential Threat to U.S. Security?

THE END of the cold war has seen a sharp decline in terrorist activities in most of the world, to the relief of nearly everyone. In the victorious coalition war against Saddam Hussein one of the chief sponsors of terrorism, Syria, actually fought on the allied side, while two other states which had long supported terrorist activities, Iran and Libya, were neutralized. Of course the war had destroyed Saddam Hussein's own fearsome terrorist machine, and severely damaged the infrastructure of such terrorist groups as the Palestine Liberation Organization, whose tentacles had once reached into Central America and the Caribbean. Now cut off from principal sources of funding such as Saudi Arabia and Kuwait, who had become fierce foes of Iraq, it is difficult to see how they can recover their pre Gulf war strength in the foreseeable future.

The Soviet Union, ruled since its inception by the Bolshevik party, which had practised terrorism from the moment of its birth at the turn of the century, had apparently ceased to encourage terrorist activities, at least discernibly, though the KGB seemed to have been left unaffected by the Gorbachev reforms. It appeared to be concentrating its energies in the post-Communist era on grappling with its intractable internal problems. Former satellite countries which specialized in training terrorists and spies, such as the old German Democratic Republic and Czechoslovakia, had of course overthrown their totalitarian regimes and, like the Soviets themselves, also turned inward to focus exclusively on problems at home.

Can it be said, then, that we live in a terror-free world? Does the KGB no longer target the United States as No. 1 on its "hit list," as it and its predecessors (under different names) had been doing since Lenin seized power in 1917? Hardly. In the "new world order" that President Bush and other Western leaders are trying to create, terrorism occupies a much lower place on their list of concerns than it did before, but it is not dead. The KGB is undeniably less of a threat to peace and freedom than it used to be, but its claws have only been sheathed not removed. Until the formerly Communist countries have embarked irreversibly on the path toward political and economic freedom, and as long as they remain in dire economic straits and political limbo, radical elements will try to seize every opportunity to portray the United States as their main enemy and employ every means to undermine it, including subversion and terror.

The United States thus appears to be no longer targeted by foreign terrorists—always excepting insane fanatics capable of staging a suicidal attack somewhere—for destabilization. On the other hand, it emerged from the war with Iraq the only superpower in the world, and though that has made it the object of universal respect it has also become, in some quarters, an object of envy and hatred. Moscow cannot be deliriously happy over the U.S. victory in Iraq.

The ebbs and flows of world affairs are not, however, the only factor to consider in evaluating whether, or to what degree, the security of the United States may be vulnerable to attack. Its long, porous borders to the north and south offer a permanent invitation to terrorists, or others who may have reason to seek its destruction or dismemberment. That is especially true of its southern flank, where it co-exists with a country, and beyond it a continent, which suffer from most of the ills of semi- or under-developed societies, and in which many kinds of subversive forces continue to flourish. We must bear in mind that the defeats of terrorists in the Old World may have little effect upon their comrades who inhabit the New World.

We have only to recall that throughout the 1980s the Sandinistas in Nicaragua were preaching "revolution without frontiers"— a clear threat to neighboring countries—and, though defeated in a democratic revolution, they still persist in their subversive activities. As one prime example, they retain control of the army and it continues to send arms to the Marxist-Leninist Farabundo Martí National Liberation Front in next-door El Salvador. The FMLN, for its part, has not ceased to sow death and destruction in Salvadoran society.

Both Central American countries are major senders of illegal immigrants to the United States.

In Colombia, the drug traffickers have formed armed militias to war against the central government, sometimes in league with various leftist guerrilla groups. The deepening ties between the Colombian narcotraficantes and their Mexican counterparts are cause for utmost concern. Mexico, as a result of the crippling of the Florida route of cocaine shipments into the United States, has virtually replaced it as the chief transshipment point for the Colombian drug cartels. In Peru, the Shining Path, perhaps the most dangerous revolutionary force south of the border, thrives on sanguinary assaults against peaceful citizens and institutions. All this is not to say that there is a readily perceived threat to U.S. or hemispheric security present in Latin America, but the potential is very much there.

That potential, thanks to a porous southern border, carries over into our own society. It inheres in the presence within the United States of a large and growing underclass of illegal aliens, whose actual total we cannot know but is calculated by immigration experts to run into several millions. (See Table 3.)

TABLE 3
Estimate of Overall Undocumented Population
as of January 1, 1990 (millions)

	Lower	Moderate	Upper
Undocumented population as of January 1, 1982	2.675	3.350	4.025
Growth: 1982 - Jan. 1, 1990	+0.8	+1.6	+2.4
Less Number Legalized	1.67	1.67	1.67
Total Population on January 1, 1990	1.805	3.280	4.755

Source: National Council of La Raza: *Unfinished Business: The Immigration Reform and Control Act of 1986.*

This alien underclass is constantly growing, for regardless of whether illegal immigration increases or decreases in any given period, and whatever the total of undocumented migrants who enter the country in any particular year, they augment the size of the underclass. Besides, its natural rate of demographic growth ensures its continued expansion.

Two other factors give cause for concern about the potential security threat that the illegals underclass may represent. One, as we saw in the previous chapter, is that it is not easily assimilable. As long as people live their lives outside the law, they will tend to keep to themselves except out of sheerest necessity, as when a job requires some contact with the mainstream of society. Even so, they automatically resume their place in the underclass the moment they arrive home from work and rejoin their families. Thus episodic contact with the mainstream does not diminish the size of the underclass.

The other factor, which points up a perennial problem, is that an illegal is by definition manipulable by forces inimical to society. We have stressed this in previous chapters. But in them, we dealt exclusively with the illegal's vulnerability to criminals; although at times violence resulted, even against law-enforcement officers, that cannot be put down as terrorism or subversion. Now it is time to discuss the problem—latent, for the moment—of the possible use of pliant illegals for terrorist or generally subversive purposes under given circumstances.

Here, we return to our concern over the porousness of the border.

Amitai Etzioni, a transplanted Israeli who is a scholar on security issues, once confessed that he could not get used to the "loose security" of his adopted country around its southern border. In a *Washington Post* piece, he wrote:

> Nobody, in my experience, mentions that able-bodied spies and terrorists may cross the Rio Grande at least with the same ease as maids seeking household work in the North. Indeed, it seems it would be quite easy to march a small division into the United States, every night, for quite a while. People who feel that I am exaggerating should note: this is happening now, only the 'divisions' want to work rather than to foment trouble.[1]

It usually takes a dramatic foreign crisis to awaken the U.S. Government—and then only temporarily—to the potential threats to its security that have appeared near its borders. The Immigration and Naturalization Service was transferred from the Labor Department to the Justice Department in 1940, just after World War II had broken out, because of heightened concern over security. Our armed forces were put on high alert during the 1962 Cuban missile crisis, the gravest direct threat ever to our society. The prospect of hostilities with Iraq following its invasion of Kuwait on August 2, 1990, resulted in tighter controls at the border and closer cooperation between INS and the FBI and other internal security agencies. Sporadic fits of concern, however, have not been matched by remedial action, such as providing greater resources for the INS and other agencies concerned with border security, or making a long-term commitment to improve border management

During past periods of political unrest in Mexico, insurgency movements and pro- and anti-regime factions have made use of safehavens in U.S. border areas to wage armed campaigns and recruit adherents. The history of past Mexican conflicts that spilled over into the United States suggests the variety of threats we could conceivably face in the future, if Mexico became unstable and the border remained neglected. Juan Nepomuceno Cortina remains an Hispanic folk hero because he dared attack Anglo lawmen in the late 1850s in the Brownsville, Texas area. More than 20 Americans and Mexicans died during the Nepomuceno raid, according to Oscar Martínez's informative account.

The Mexican Revolution of 1910 provoked serious conflict in the U.S. borderlands. As Martínez notes:

> Mexico's civil unrest not only brought injury and property loss to Americans who lived south of the boundary, but the ferment also spilled over into Texas, New Mexico, Arizona and California, spawning a strong reaction among the Anglo border population. The unstable climate set the stage for repeated incursions of Mexican revolutionaries and bandits into U.S. territory and punitive or 'defensive' movements by American troops into Mexico. Such events produced repeated violent incidents along the entire border.... The most tragic clashes occurred in 1915-16 in the lower Río Grande Valley, when adherents of the 'Plan de San Diego,' a document that called for Mexican insurgency in the Southwest, repeatedly raided Texas settlements.[2]

The ultimate price the United States paid for its unprotected southern flank was Pancho Villa's sacking of the border town of Columbus, New Mexico, in 1916, during which eighteen Americans were killed.

A more recent example of Mexican extremists entering the United States and attempting to use ethnic communities was cited by the late Congressman Larry P. McDonald, in a statement he inserted in the *Congressional Record*. In it, he referred to the reported use of United States territory as a safe haven from Mexican authorities by the Mexican terrorist group *Liga Communista 23 de Septiembre*, in the late 1970s.

In his monograph for the London Centre for Security and Conflict Studies in 1986, Samuel Francis relates what the Liga was up to:

> The LC-23 has been visibly active in organizing among Mexican citizens along the U.S. border such as at Juárez. There the LC-23 has been particularly active in supporting illegal entry into the United States and has organized large concerted border 'invasions' by gangs of illegal immigrants.[3]

By 1977, the LC-23 had some 600 members, and they had murdered more than 100 Mexican police officers and participated in the kidnapping of a British Honorary Consul in Mexico, Francis reports further. Among their activities in the United States was a close relationship with the Socialist Workers Party, the leading Trotskyite group, which sought to obtain refugee status for an LC-23 founder, Héctor Marroquín Manríquez. Marroquín had been arrested by the U.S. Border Patrol as he attempted to enter the United States.

As the experience of the Mexican Revolution clearly shows, it is during a time of internal upheaval when our southern neighbor becomes rife with extremist agitation. Given a background of resentment-cum-fear of the United States, the agitators almost invariably appeal to anti-Yankee sentiment—under guise of "anti-imperialism"—though anti-Americanism is more the artificial creation of an elite jealously protective of its own prerogatives than a popular phenomenon. Mexican intellectuals resorted precisely to that appeal early in the debate, in 1990 and 1991, over the prospect of a U.S.-Mexico Free Trade Agreement: They railed against the supposed threat of domination of the Mexican economy by U.S. multinational corporations, while deriding the probability that free trade would benefit Mexico's working population.

Fortunately, the economic reforms of President Carlos Salinas de Gortari have laid some groundwork for serious improvement of his people's living standards, though the reforms have so far been limited. The Free Trade Agreement can expand that basis by encouraging not only the unimpeded flow of goods and services   between the two countries but also large-scale U.S. and other for-   eign investment in productive business enterprises, which in turn would create new jobs for Mexicans, augment their purchasing power, and discourage emigration. Meanwhile, however, Mexico's economic plight remains serious. It might take perhaps a decade or more, believe some analysts, before the combined effects of Salinas's reforms and FTA trickle down to the people. Until that happens, Mexico's potential for exporting illegals will remain great, and so will, concomitantly, their potential for getting into or creating trouble for the United States.

***

Terrorists or subversives might take advantage of the "loose security" that reigns at the border, in at least three ways:

1. They could slip across the Río Grande to carry out hit-and-run attacks against Americans or American property.

2. They could opt for quietly establishing safehouses in the country, looking more to future than present objectives. The Soviets, and before them the Nazis, proved adept at establishing safehouses in strategic locations and putting them to good use. These can be used to raise funds, build support groups, or even store weapons—all important tools for the conduct of terrorist or covert political operations within the United States or in other countries nearby not excluding Mexico itself.

3. They would almost certainly seek to utilize the large communities of illegal aliens already in the United States, particularly those who might feel isolated or perceive cultural, racial,

religious, or economic discrimination against them. They could be turned into sympathetic or supportive subcultures to obtain political or logistical support for their movements, or to suppress dissenters in their midst.

Although the United States has remained relatively free of terrorist incidents during the past two decades, compared with Europe and the Middle East, that is not cause for complacency. Many documented cases are on record of third country terrorists and political operatives who entered the country illegally to conduct clandestine operations.

Samuel Francis reports that on July 16, 1978, Kris Berster, a member of the Baader-Meinhof Gang who was wanted on criminal and terrorist charges in West Germany, was arrested by the U.S. Border Patrol as she attempted to cross the U.S.-Canadian border at Alburg, Vermont, while using a false Iranian passport. The day following her arrest, three individuals who were believed to have been associated with Berster returned to Canada after attempting to enter the United States at the same point, and after being questioned by the U.S. Border Patrol.

Francis also reports this incident:

> In January 1986, Mexican authorities informed the INS that four Libyans carrying large sums of money had arrived in Mexico City after a complex journey from Beirut through Geneva, Amsterdam, and Panama City. The Mexicans deported the Libyans to Panama. Shortly after, the INS apprehended three suspected terrorists of undisclosed nationality who attempted to enter the United States through El Paso and Atlanta.[4]

In 1988, the FBI sought an indictment in Virginia against Saleh Al-Rajhi, who ostensibly worked on Libyan student matters, for gathering information on U.S. intelligence agencies for the Libyan Government. He had entered the U.S. illegally in 1984, reported the *Washington Post*'s Carlyle Murphy, who specializes in the Middle East.[5]

A high FBI official told a Senate subcommittee in 1989 that terrorists associated with Iran's Revolutionary Guard had infiltrated the United States and could be used to carry out death threats ordered by top Iranian revolutionary leaders, reported the *Washington Times*'s

Bill Gertz. The official, FBI Executive Associate Director Oliver B. Revell, added that large numbers of Iranian students in the United States, many of them here illegally, are "zealous adherents of the Khomeini rhetoric... and pursuit of violence." Revell said that porous U.S. borders and lenient State Department visa restrictions have made it difficult for the FBI to track terrorists who may be motivated to conduct terrorist actions in support of Iran, Gertz added.[6]

In a 1989 report on the increasing numbers of aliens crossing the Southwest border illegally, and then claiming political asylum, government affairs specialist Charles Phillips wrote in the *American Legion* magazine:

> The U.S. intelligence community is concerned about the possibility, if not probability, that the aliens arriving from Communist countries include spies, saboteurs and terrorists. Among the Cuban boat people in 1980, for example, were an estimated 18,000 single men of military age. Intelligence sources believe at least some of them were trained guerrilla specialists of the Castro regime.[7]

Fortunately, the Cuban arrivals proved to be law-abiding. It is nothing short of miraculous that the United States has escaped egregious acts of terrorism like, for example, the cruel murder of Italian Prime Minister Aldo Moro. The bombing of Pan Am Flight 103 near Lockerbie, Scotland, was of course directed against the United States; but it was not committed in U.S. air space. Yet the targets in our country are many and most of them obvious.

The "mother of all atrocities," to play on Saddam Hussein's promise to wage the "mother of all battles" against the UN coalition, is without doubt the torching of more than 500 Kuwaiti oil wells. That caused unspeakable horror for other Middle East countries besides Kuwait, for the billows of smoke arising from the fired wells darkened the skies for hundreds of square miles and transformed day into perpetual night for all living things in the region. The firefighters called in to put out the blazing fires estimated that it would take up to two years, perhaps longer, to accomplish the task. The region's ecology, however, may never fully recover.

The Kuwait tragedy brings to mind an interview with the Houston District Commissioner of the INS, Paul B. O'Neill, in 1986.

At that time, a San Diego TV station had reported that Muammar Quaddafi, the Libyan dictator and sponsor of terrorism, threatened to unleash terrorists on the San Diego naval base, second largest in the nation. O'Neill and other INS officials in the region were on a state of alert, watching for Middle East aliens entering the country from Mexico who might look suspicious. He told me:

> Quaddafi scares the hell out of me. We are one of the biggest petroleum centers in the world. We have petrochemical companies, refineries, storage tanks, what have you. So if he had in mind to hurt our oil industry, he would come to Houston.[8]

Times have changed. Quaddafi was laid low by a U.S. air strike that nearly destroyed his command center. Enter Saddam Hussein. He was disposed of in the 100-hour ground war that left his country in ruins. But before departing the world stage, he made sure that Kuwait would be turned into a raging inferno. That recalled O'Neill's parting warning, at the end of our interview: "Sooner or later, [terrorism] is going to happen [here, in Houston]."[9]

We all devoutly pray that terrorism will never strike Houston or any other American city. But forewarned is forearmed. Of 144 terrorist acts committed or attempted in the United States between 1981 and 1985, 84, or some 60 percent, were carried out by organizations associated with foreign ethnic or nationality groups, reports Samuel Francis. They included groups as varied as Libyans, Armenians, Iranians, anti-Castro Cubans, and Indian Sikhs. The number of terrorists and extremists among large ethnic minority communities can only be tiny, on the whole. But a mere two or three such persons can cause extensive damage. It took only three Puerto Rican terrorists, in 1954, to shoot up the U.S. Congress and make an attempt on President Harry Truman's life.

They were motivated by perceived grievances against the United States, which they alleged had kept Puerto Rico in bondage as a "colony" since 1898, when we defeated Spain in war and took the island. We maintained it as a protectorate until 1952 when, by mutual consent of the United States and the Puerto Rican Government, which was headed for the first time by a native Puerto Rican, it was declared the "Commonwealth of Puerto Rico" and granted virtually all the rights of a state. Nevertheless, fanatical *independentistas* have been committing acts of terrorism ever since, including bombings of U.S. Navy vehicles and planes on the island itself and of federal buildings in New York City and Chicago.

A similar pattern could show up in Mexico if that country's government is unable to resolve its decade-long crisis. In the event, Mexicans who are fed up with bad conditions at home could, in an effort to draw worldwide attention to their plight, perpetrate acts of terror against American nationals in Mexico and/or American lives and property on U.S. territory. The sheer size of the illegal flow would make it extraordinarily difficult for Mexico's security agencies to halt such acts, even did they possess the political will to do so. U.S. agencies, chronically undermanned, would be helpless.

12

What Should Be Done About Illegal Immigration?

ILLEGAL IMMIGRATION from Mexico will grow in volume in the coming decades. It is also likely to become an increasing burden, and even a source of disruption, for many U.S. municipalities and states. That is the consensus among immigration experts, supported by the realities and the scientific projections based on them. The economic and demographic forces that stimulate illegal immigration, and the social networks and expectations that sustain it, are too deeply rooted to warrant any other prognosis.

Assuming the validity of that prognosis, illegal immigration is bound to become a national issue which will ultimately require the constant attention of the highest levels of the U.S. Government. U.S. leaders, including the President himself, must be aware of the consequences to our society if measures are not taken to deal with it realistically. But at present, under the pressure of other seemingly more important problems, foreign as well as domestic, their inclination seems to be to sweep the illegals question under the carpet. In the end that will only enhance its potential for damage to society.

The major factor that sustains illegal migration will continue to be Mexico's population growth—despite a lower rate than a decade ago—and the even more rapid expansion of its working age population. The "pull" factor of jobs in the United States is basically secondary; what is primary is the "push" of poverty and massive unemployment/underemployment in Mexico that drives people north regardless of the availability of jobs in the United States. The pull factor is, however, reinforced by durable networks of families and friends which have an attraction all their own. (This may be, in

116

the opinion of some experts, more powerful than the conventional push-pull syndrome motivated by demographic/economic forces.)

Mexico's economy shows signs of improvement after a decade of crisis, but it has not risen much above the level of stagnation caused by the crisis. Although economic growth rates are positive, they are only slightly above the population rate of increase. Worst of all, the reduction by about half in the standard of living that the average Mexican enjoyed in 1982, when the crisis broke out, has not been restored.

Economic output and job creation have been stimulated by the twin policies of the Salinas Administration to open Mexico wider to international trade and investment—especially through a free trade agreement with the United States and Canada—and to shrink the state's hold upon the economy. Two countervailing factors may, however, stall recovery in its tracks.

One is the recession in the United States and other industrial countries. Its effects may spread to Mexico and/or hinder U.S. efforts to spark Mexican development through such means as the Free Trade Agreement, private investment, and further debt reduction assistance. It will require a lengthy transitional period for FTA to stimulate uninterrupted production growth and exports, before it can take hold and yield palpable benefits for the people of both countries, particularly impoverished Mexicans.

More important in the long term, Salinas's reforms are not yet deep enough to propel a sustained upward movement in production, nor are they guaranteed permanence and irreversibility—a matter of utmost concern. Salinas leaves office in December 1994, and may be a lame duck during most of his last year. Mexicans are understandably preoccupied with these questions: What if his reforms fail because they fall short of what is required? Does he have the time and the will to make further and deeper reforms? And what—this is the key question—if his successor slows down, or worse, reverses the reforms he has instituted?

The nub of the problem is that under Mexico's political system the President is virtually all powerful, and can alter decisively the course of events simply by a stroke of the pen. That is exactly what Salinas himself did when he abruptly reversed the nationalization of the country's private banks, which a predecessor had decreed only eight years earlier. The Mexican system lacks the accountability to which a chief executive is held in Western democracies. It does not provide for checks and balances, which require the judiciary or the legislature, or both, to intervene to make the executive accountable for its acts and policies. In fact, those two institutions are but instruments of the ruling Institutional Revolutionary Party. A graphic example of that was the 1982 bank nationalization itself. Though President José López Portillo's *ukase* violated the Constitution, it was not struck down by the Supreme Court, whose justices are all PRI appointees and dutifully carry out the President's will, while the big PRI majority in Congress supinely approved it *ex post facto*.

Many Americans and Mexicans hope, and none more than the U.S. Government, that the Mexico-U.S. Free Trade Agreement will help institutionalize Salinas's reforms, thus perhaps precluding any effort to reverse them, and at the same time foster major foreign investment to increase economic production. But since it will take some years—as many as fifteen years, some trade experts estimate— to become fully operative, FTA may not be able to do much more than initiate those processes and leave it to Salinas's successor to develop them further. In any event, his reform program still has far to go.

For one thing, his privatization effort has barely scratched the surface: The process of dismantling the state enterprises that control the economy is, as we have seen in the former socialist countries in Eastern Europe and in the Soviet Union itself, slow, arduous and fraught with serious political obstacles. Salinas, for all his courage and foresight, has so far not dared to privatize the "strategic"—i. e., basic—state enterprises, above all Petróleos Mexicanos, by far the country's biggest industry and the heart of its economy. Nor has he attempted to privatize other "strategic" parastatals which, though less important than PEMEX, are also basic to economic growth, such as the railroads, electric power, and a food processing-supermarket chain which is subsidized by the state and competes with private companies. Mexico's economic infrastructure, in short, remains essentially in state hands, and as long as it does the development of a free-market economy, and the creation of enough jobs to absorb annual additions to the labor force, will be seriously hampered.

Thus Mexico's chronic job deficit is not likely to vanish soon, even under the most optimistic growth scenarios. Mexico's officially proclaimed unemployment rate for 1991 of only 2.3 percent is seriously misleading. The rate is based on periodic surveys of certain industries in a small number of major cities. Anyone who had worked at all—however briefly—in the period of the survey, was considered employed. But many of those in fact qualified as underemployed, or would be counted as unemployed under U.S. employment counting methods. The best estimates put unemployment/underemployment at somewhere between 40 and 50 percent of the workforce.

Mexico's labor force will grow at a 3.1 percent annual rate in the 1990s (see Table 4), bringing one million new jobseekers into the labor market each year. The total could be even larger if Mexico's women, influenced by modernization, decide to participate in the workforce at a rate closer to that of women in Western industrial countries.

TABLE 4
Mexico's Population and Labor Force Growth: 1990-2010
(millions)

	1990	1995	2000	2005	2010
Total Population	88.6	98.0	107.2	116.3	125.2
Total Labor Force	31.2	35.9	40.4	45.1	49.8
Labor Force, Male	22.7	25.9	29.1	32.3	35.4
Labor Force, Female	8.5	10.0	11.3	12.8	14.4
Labor Force, Agric.	9.4	9.6	9.7	9.4	9.0
Labor Force, Urban	21.8	26.3	30.7	35.7	40.8

Source: United Nations World Population Assessment, 1990

The net new additions to the labor force will exceed one million in the first decade of the 21st century, according to the projections made by Bouvier and Simcox. Only after 2010 will this rapid growth slow, they add, as the lower birth rates of the end of the century begin to be reflected in the size of the working age population.[1]

To reduce unemployment to current Western European levels by the year 2000, Mexico's economy would have to create on the order of 1.3 million jobs a year—one million to provide for new entrants to the labor force, plus 300,000 to absorb the existing pool of unemployed and underemployed. Such a performance would represent job growth of a hefty 6 percent yearly. Few economies have performed so prodigiously over a sustained period. The United States, with far greater capital and technological resources, increased employment by only 2-3 percent a year during the expansionary Reagan period— the best job-creation performance of all the Western industrial countries.

Mexico's development strategy in recent decades has stressed inputs of capital over labor, its most abundant resource. Emphasis on more labor-intensive production to absorb workers presents a dilemma in dealing with migration pressures. Many of those immigrating illegally into the United States have jobs of some sort in Mexico, and by accepted standards they would qualify as underemployed. They leave because those jobs are irregular and low-paid, with hourly earnings as little as one-tenth of the U.S. minimum wage. The prospect of making much more money in the United States is a powerful lure to immigrants. It will remain so, particularly in labor-intensive industries where remuneration will necessarily be relatively lower, even as Mexico increases its industrial employment.

Other factors will also continue to spur immigration. Because of a deficient public education system, many of Mexico's workers are unskilled and seriously undereducated. They will continue to be more suitable for unskilled labor in U.S. perishable crop agriculture and the services sector than for the new jobs in Mexico's emerging industries.

Not all the forces driving people to migrate illegally to the United States are economic, though that is the primary motivation. Illegal immigration has gone through stages where it becomes a cumulative, self-nourishing process. The rapid growth of the Mexican population in major U.S. cities during the last two decades has steadily expanded the kinship and job networks that, in turn, stimulate others to come. They are drawn not only by jobs, but also the prospect of rejoining family members or gaining access to better schools and public services, as Seth Mydans reported in the *New York Times*. [2]

The Mexican analyst, Luis Horacio Durán, believes that the "desire for achievement" may be the "most important factor" that draws Mexican workers northward. He makes this novel point:

> When the Mexican worker returns to his own country, family, friends, neighbors, he will feel proud if he can tell [them] and prove a history of success working in the United States.
>
> It may seem strange, but when the worker performs a task in the United States with quality, with discipline, he is not only looking for economic reward but is [also] trying to prove to himself and others (thousands of miles away) that he is capable of being a success outside his own country. [3]

So the incentives and rewards for illegal immigration have multiplied, while many of the disincentives have weakened. U.S. laws and court decisions have reduced barriers to public services and assistance for illegal immigrants (see *Doe v. Plyler*, 1982). A number of states grant resident tuition rates to illegal aliens attending state colleges, while U.S. citizens and legal residents from neighboring states continue paying the higher out-of-state rates.

IRCA's amnesty provisions sent a clear signal to many prospective illegals: Get into the United States, settle down, and ultimately you will be allowed to stay. Mexican-American advocacies have been lobbying for another amnesty ever since, as we have noted, and now press for the legalization of thousands who arrived illegally after the 1982 cutoff date of the last amnesty. Later, they can be expected to favor legalization after yet another cutoff date. And so on and on, instituting a process of "rolling amnesty" ad infinitum.

The employer sanctions enacted in 1986 as the main deterrent to illegal immigration did indeed deter it significantly for two years. INS apprehensions fell by one-third in 1987, then dropped to well below a million in 1988 and 1989. There is little doubt, according to a 1990 study by the Urban Institute, that Mexicans hoping to cross the border believed the sanctions would work and therefore chose to stay home.[4] By 1989, however, word had reached them that false work authorization documents and other stratagems to beat the law were easily available, and that vitiated the law's deterrent effect. In addition, the Reagan and Bush administrations failed to carry out the major increases in Border Patrol strength provided in the 1986 law.

**

What can be done to slow down appreciably, if not halt altogether, the flow of illegals into this country? The simple, but not very operational answer is to make Mexico a better place to live and work in, and to make the United States less congenial to illegal settlers.

For decades, Mexican leaders have promised that economic development would eventually end the need of their citizens to migrate to El Norte, as Cardoso has reported in his study.[5] In the course of those years, both Americans and Mexicans have developed a great body of literature on how to stimulate Mexico's economy to provide jobs for all who want them. One of the most recent and most ambitious studies is the Report of the Commission for the Study of International Migration and Cooperative Economic Development, *Unauthorized Migration: An Economic Development Response*, issued in 1990. The Commission, chaired by Diego C. Asencio, a retired Foreign Service Officer who has been ambassador to Brazil and Colombia, was established by Congress in the 1986 Immigration Reform and Control Act, with this unusual mandate:

> The Commission . . . shall examine the conditions in Mexico and such other sending countries which contribute to unauthorized migration to the United States and (shall explore) mutually beneficial, reciprocal trade and investment programs to alleviate such conditions.[6]

The Commission's recommendations were enlightened and carefully drawn. They called for generally desirable and sound actions by the U.S. Government, international lending and assistance agencies, and U.S. and international private enterprise. Leading the list were recommendations for a U.S.-Mexico Free Trade Agreement, a border development and cooperation commission, more foreign assistance for Mexico's family planning program, more AID funding for education, debt restructuring, stimulation of small business development, and encouragement of maquiladoras and manufactured exports.

Most of the Commission's recommendations make good sense and would, if carried out, advance important interests of the United States and a sound international order. But their efficacy in producing an early reduction of illegal immigration is doubtful. The Commission Report itself acknowledged that the effect on migration would be long in coming:

> .... the development process itself tends to stimulate migration in the short to medium term by raising expectations and enhancing peoples' ability to migrate. Thus, the development solution to unauthorized migration is measured in decades—even generations.[7]

Regrettably, while dwelling in great detail upon what the United States should do the Commission was reluctant to make suggestions for Mexican action, though the immigration problem is clearly bilateral. It made no mention of the need to severely curtail official corruption and excessive political and economic centralization in Mexico, and to remove fundamental obstacles to private investment which have restricted job creation and encouraged the country's grave maldistribution of income. As for immigration policy, the Commission Report ignored Mexico's long-standing, if unstated policy of welcoming emigration northward as a "safety valve"— in the exact phrase used by Mexican officials in private— to relieve persistent social and economic pressures at home which might otherwise erupt in popular outbreaks.

President Salinas has often stated that Mexico wants to export goods, not people. He might begin with promulgating a counter-emigration policy of encouraging people to stay home by granting them title to farmland over which the state exercises dominion under its agrarian reform. More than 200 million acres of land under government control in the form of *ejidos* — a type of collective — are notoriously underproductive, and have contributed to a chronic agricultural crisis which forces Mexico to import food and grains costing billions of dollars annually it can ill afford. The President might follow up by taking legal steps to install a regime of private property across the board, giving each Mexican a stake in his own country through fostering private ownership of the means of production. It is axiomatic that no human being with a solid stake in his country would willingly abandon it.

Finally, Salinas should deepen and accelerate the pace of his economic reforms and couple them with parallel changes in the country's obsolete authoritarian political system—in short, hasten Mexico's "modernization," as he frequently characterizes his program. Of course this requires that he push as hard for democratization of the political system as he has for liberalization of the economy.

Both supporters and opponents of the Mexico-U.S. FTA argued for such democratization in the debate, during the first half of 1991, over extending the "fast-track" procedure to authorize President Bush to negotiate an FTA with Mexico. A total of 37 Members of Congress co-signed a letter to President Bush which virtually demanded that the Mexicans institute "sweeping changes"—as the letter put it—in their political system, as a condition for joining in a trade partnership with their northern neighbor. Though to make such a demand was implicitly interventionist, since Mexico is after all a sovereign country which enjoys the right to order its own house, and therefore it could not properly be included in a formal trade agreement, the signers' concern was shared by most Americans and by Mexican democrats. That concern will grow, rather than diminish, as the FTA moves ahead. If Salinas is unwilling, or unable, to press forward with democratization, he will come under the greatest pressure to do so in the remaining years of his Presidency both from within and without.

The U.S. Government must also exert pressure upon Mexico with regard to modernization as well as immigration, which are interlinked bilateral issues. It cannot afford to lag behind the public and the Congress in addressing the illegals problem. If for no other reason, to passively await long-term economic and political reforms in Mexico would be to acquiesce in spreading social ills and rising public assistance costs in the Southwest, along with the continued growth of a socially aggrieved and, increasingly in the future, politically alienated underclass.

What, concretely, should the Administration do?

First and foremost, it must acknowledge the seriousness of the illegals problem and accord it the highest priority possible. It will do little good to spend endless amounts of time, energy, and money on the near-hopeless task of mediating conflicts elsewhere in the world if, in the end, the price will be to neglect a festering problem within our own society which carries the potential for generating grave internal conflict.

President Bush is known and admired for his understanding and compassionate attitude toward Mexico and its problems. He has spent much time cultivating the friendship and understanding of his Mexican counterpart, Carlos Salinas, a leader not known until his accession to power for his cordial attitude toward Yankees. The chemistry between them has been good. The coincidence of both men presiding over their respective countries at the same time has been fortunate and unique. That came out during the official visit of President Bush to Monterrey in November 1990, when, to the surprise of skeptical observers who have seen manipulated displays of Mexican hospitality before, plain citizens repeatedly hailed their distinguished visitor with spontaneous joy. The "new era of friendship" between the two neighbors which their heads of state inaugurated in Monterrey was quite credible.

It is doubtful that we shall witness again, in the foreseeable future, so profound an affinity between the leaders of both neighboring countries. This is the time to take fullest advantage of a fortunate coincidence. In this, George Bush must take the initiative. He must, first of all, separate in his own mind the personal admiration and respect he holds for Salinas from the harsh realities of conditions in Mexico; they demand that a more vigorous effort be undertaken to effectuate radical change. Without such a clear definition of where he stands, it is difficult to imagine Bush tackling the illegals problem with all the power at his command.

The Congress-appointed Commission for the Study of International Migration and Cooperative Economic Development, which issued the report on "unauthorized migration" noted above, recommended the creation of an Agency for Migration Affairs to handle all immigration matters. Its motive, to give the issue "a high priority on the U.S. domestic and foreign policy agendas," is laudable. But past experience, especially where Mexico has figured importantly, shows that such new agencies tend to overlap existing ones and only result in adding bureaucratic complications to an already labyrinthine snarl. Besides, a coherent policy must be framed before it can be determined that a new agency is needed.

In addition to the friendly pressure the Administration must exert upon Mexico to bring about real modernization as rapidly as possible, it must simultaneously pursue three other lines of action. These are:

• Attenuate the "pull" factors — the signals U.S. society sends that encourage people to settle here illegally.

IRCA's enforcement centerpiece was, to repeat, employer sanctions, which aimed at turning off the magnet of jobs luring illegal aliens here. That key feature has not been allowed to fulfill its deterrent potential.

To reduce the exploitation of illegal aliens as well as discourage their employment, there must be a much stronger commitment to enforcement of wage-and-hour and industrial safety laws by state and federal governments, concentrating on regions and industries where use of illegal workers is widespread.

Current laws and regulations barring illegal aliens from expensive public assistance and services, such as welfare and food stamps, must be strengthened and extended. Valuable public privileges, such as drivers' permits and occupational licenses, should be denied to them—a practice now in effect in some states.

Above all, the U.S. Government must send signals that it considers illegal immigration a pernicious social evil it is determined to eradicate. Proposals for additional amnesties are a beckoning call to would-be illegals: they strengthen the impression we don't take our own laws seriously. Such proposals must be rejected.

• Strengthen border controls and other deterrents.

Many Americans are reluctant to even talk about policing the border effectively. It seems to go against the humanitarian instincts and the openness of our society, and implies distrust, hostility even, toward our southern neighbor.

But as the clandestine traffic of Mexicans northward has swelled, the border, particularly where major urban areas intersect, has become an increasingly dangerous place. The Mexican authorities seem to agree.

The Mexican Consul General in San Diego, Enrique Loeza, has stated publicly that after nine months in his job he received "an impression that there was rising tension in the area," as he told the *New York Times*.[8] He added that a special Mexican unit to combat bandits had detained 550 people in its first six months of operation. This did curtail some violence against Mexicans by Mexicans. Nevertheless, Loeza felt that enough violent incidents had occurred to make for "rising tension in the area."

The INS has reported a persistent increase in assaults on Border Patrol agents in recent years. In FY 1989 (October 1988-September 1989), it counted 164 agents assaulted in 117 incidents. In FY 1990, the totals were 363 and 294, respectively—both record highs. There seemed little letup in FY 1991, judging by INS figures for the first quarter, for which it reported 50 assaults on agents and 42 incidents.

Rock-throwing has become the preferred assault weapon against Border Patrol agents—a kind of *intifada*. In FY 1989, only 14 percent of weapons used against them were rocks, but in 1990 the total had risen to 41 percent and in the first quarter of 1991 it was 32 percent. This represented an increase of 151 percent in the use of rocks, compared with only 9 percent use of firearms in assaults. One could rationalize that the attackers' intent was not, at least, to kill; but whatever the nature of their weapons they contributed to a growing lawlessness along the border.

Here is a graphic description of the situation by one veteran agent, as reported by Steven García of the AFL-CIO's National Border Patrol Council:

During the hours of daylight the border area is relatively serene and desolate. Under the cover of darkness, however, literally thousands of people gather in small and large groups, intent on entering the U.S. through the canyons along the (San Diego area) border. The incredible volume of traffic in such a small area creates an atmosphere which is frustrating and at times frightening. Hostile crowds of people hurl rocks, bottles, and insults at Border Patrol Agents who venture close to the border.

I have had innumerable rocks thrown at me, and I have seen agents seriously injured by rocks, which are potentially lethal weapons. The rocks that are thrown are not pebbles; they are large stones which are hurled at the velocity of baseballs.

Along that same 12-mile stretch of border in San Diego during 1988, 99 incidents of rock assaults were recorded against Border Patrol Agents, with 21 enforcement vehicle windshields and windows destroyed. In 1989, there were 229 recorded rock assaults. . . there are more than a few Border Patrol Agents who carry scars from being struck by rocks, with several agents suffering permanent sensory damage from rock barrages.[9]

A provision of the 1990 Immigration Act (PL 101-649) increases the Border Patrol by 1,000, to more than 5,000 positions. Assuming the cash-strapped executive branch eventually funds the increase (it failed to deliver fully on major increases legislated in 1986), the Border Patrol's resources will still not match the demands imposed on it.

As the GAO reports, in recent years the Border Patrol has acquired additional law enforcement missions, mainly drug interdiction and location of criminal aliens, for which it has received few new resources. To be fully effective in meeting its expanding drug interdiction mission while curbing illegal entries and border crime, and indeed even protecting itself in an increasingly hostile environment, the Border Patrol should have at least 6,000 agents deployed on the Canadian and Mexican borders and other major ports of entry, with adequate vehicles and aircraft and high-tech detection hardware.

Other necessary deterrents include:

1. Better fences and barriers strategically placed along the 200 miles of the border where 90 percent of apprehensions of illegal aliens occur, to channel travelers into legitimate ports of entry. Consideration should be given to the proposal of the Federation of American

Immigration Reform to erect fencing in major urban areas such as San Diego, Nogales, El Paso, Del Río, and Laredo. (See Figure 2).[10]

Such deterrents will hardly wall off the United States, as some critics seem to think. It has perhaps the most open border in the world and it will remain so. There are now 29 official immigration ports of entry available to legitimate travelers along an extent of 2,000 miles, and additional ones are under consideration. In 1989, a quarter of a billion persons, 60 percent of them aliens, entered the United States freely through legal border crossing points. Such a huge traffic hardly suggests undue restriction of the legitimate movement of goods and human beings.

2. Federal prosecutors must show greater vigor in prosecuting serious immigration offenses. Aliens re-entering the United States illegally after being deported are committing a felony. Yet U.S. Attorneys, feeling the competing demands of other serious offenses, prosecute few such offenders. Alien smugglers— coyotes—account for a sizable proportion of the illegal aliens entering the country. Though many are apprehended, most cases are plea-bargained to lesser offenses or dismissed altogether. Many of the smugglers are soon back in business after forfeiting vehicles or paying modest fines. Recent legislation raising the penalties for use or fabrication of false documents also merit prosecutorial attention.

3. Closer cooperation with Mexico in combating abuses on its side of the border such as alien smuggling, counterfeiting of American ID documents, and illegal migration of Central Americans to the United States across its territory. Mexico is already doing much to curb Central American illegals, but in its anxiety to move them out of its territory it does not always favor deporting them but finds it expedient to let them slip across the Río Grande.

• Encourage rapid assimilation, with the goal of full citizenship, among Mexican nationals and their children who are here to stay.

Easy illegal immigration has brought many Mexicans here to stay. Most of the 2.5 million who came before 1982 have received temporary resident status under the 1986 amnesty, and are on their

way to full permanent resident status (though not without experiencing difficulties). Still others have come illegally since 1982.
Despite our best enforcement efforts and enlightened trade and
investment policies toward Mexico, some will continue to arrive
without authorization. Many will regard themselves as sojourners,
but recent research shows that an increasing number of illegals arrive
in America with the intention of staying.

For those who are clearly here to stay, and for their children,
U.S. society must encourage their assimilation and participation in
society. School districts in major areas of immigrant settlement must
be adequately funded, and parental participation in the schooling
process encouraged and rewarded. Instruction in Spanish in those
districts should serve as a bridge for limited English proficiency
students, if they are to make the transition to full competence in
English, the language of maximum social mobility and participation.

The U.S. and state governments, along with civic and philan-
thropic groups, should provide support and education for naturalization and voter registration campaigns and participation in American
civic life. But the country should not ease the requirements for
knowledge of English and U.S. civic practices now needed for naturalization. The United States, through its nationality laws, should
discourage the use of dual nationality and strictly enforce the bans
against naturalized citizens of Mexican origin voting in Mexican
elections (even by absentee ballot) or holding public office in
Mexico.

All levels of government should encourage a more even
distribution of Mexican immigrants around the United States,
although the difficulties that presents are many and great. Still,
enlightened education, employment, and public assistance policies
can help considerably.

But without major remedial policies the illegals problem
could assume staggering proportions. As many as three million of
them might seek permanent haven in the United States during the
1990s, along with one million more Mexicans who will arrive
legally. The immigration flow from south of the border could be even
greater in the first decade of the next century, when Mexico's labor
force growth will crest. If past settlement patterns persist, nearly two-

thirds will reside in just two states, California and Texas. Such high concentrations can perpetuate the enclave mentality of the barrio and become a major challenge to the absorptive capacity of those states.

Our success in curbing illegal immigration, on the one hand, while accelerating the assimilation of those who do manage to settle here without authorization, will determine whether many of them will be recruited into a growing and isolated foreign underclass. Now caught between ambivalent feelings about their mother country and a sense of alienation and resentment toward U.S. society, assimilation would free them of that burden along with others.

As it enters he 21st century, the United States must become internationally competitive while enlarging and protecting its democratic institutions. To meet the challenge, it will be more than ever in need of citizens and residents who are productive, healthy, law-abiding, involved in their communities, and fully committed to the American experiment. In that way, the American Dream can be fulfilled, remaining the beacon it has always been for less fortunate peoples throughout the globe.

Appendix A

Categories of Aliens Excluded Under Section 212 of the Immigration Act of 1990

Excluded are aliens who

1) are mentally retarded; 2) are insane; 3) have had one or more attacks of insanity; 4) are afflicted with psychopathic personality, sexual deviation, or a mental defect; 5) are narcotic drug addicts or chronic alcoholics; 6) are afflicted with dangerous contagious diseases; 7) are from any of the foregoing categories and whose ailments are of such a nature that they may affect their ability to earn a living; 8) are paupers, prfessional beggars, or vagrants; 9) have been convicted of a crime involving moral turpitude; 10) have been convicted of two or more offenses for which sentences or confinement have aggregated five years or more; 11) are polygamists; 12) are prostitutes or procurers; 13) are coming to the United States to engage in any immoral sexual acts; 14) are seeking to enter the U.S. to per-form skilled or unskilled labor without labor certifications; 15) are likely to become public charges; 16) have been excluded from admission and deported; 17) have been arrested and deported; 18) are stowaways; 19) have sought to procure visas by fraud or by misrepresenting material facts; 20) at the time of application for admission are not in possession of valid passports or travel documents; 21) have visas that have not been issued in compliance with the specified country numerical limitations; 22) are ineligible for citizenship; 23) are convicted of violations of U.S. or foreign controlled substance laws, or who have been illicit traffickers in such controlled substances; 24) arrive on non-complying transportation carriers; 25) are over sixteen years of age and cannot read and understand some language or dialect; 26) are not in possession of valid passports; 27) seek to enter the United States to engage in activities prejudicial to the public interest or security of the U.S.; 28) are anarchists, Communists, or members

134

of other totalitarian parties, or who seek the violent overthrow of the Government of the United States; 29) would, after entry, engage in activities which would be prohibited by the United States relating to espionage, sabotage, public disorder or other subversive activities; 30) while accompanying other aliens who are excluded and deported would have their protection or guardianship required by the aliens so deported: 31) knowingly and for gain have assisted other aliens to enter the U.S. in violation of law; 32) are graduates of medical schools not accredited by the Secretary of Education and who are coming to the United States principally to perform services as members of the medical profession; 33) have Nazi associations which participated in the persecution of others because of race, religion, national origin, or political opinion.

Appendix B

The principal violations of law involving offenses connected with illegal immigration to the United States are as follows:

8 USC 1325   Entry without inspection or use of false and misleading representation:
1) Misdemeanor, 6 months and $500
2) Subsequent convictions: Felony, up to 2 years and $ 1,000

8 USC 1326   Reentry after deportation: Felony, up to 2 years and $ 8,000

8 USC 1327   Aiding or assisting certain aliens to enter: Felony, 5 years and $8,000

8 USC 1324   Bringing in and harboring: Fine and 5 years

18 USC 1546   Fraud in obtaining visas or other documents, forgery, counterfeiting, misuse, impersonation, sale of valid visa: Fine and two years

50 USC 450   Requirement to register for Selective Service (ages 18-26): $ 25,000 fine and five years

Sources

Chapter 1

1. Tim W. Ferguson, "Californians on Edge at the Mexican Border," *Wall Street Journal*, August 23, 1990.
2. William Branigin, "Violence, Tensions Increasing Along the U.S.-Mexican Border," *Washington Post*, June 25, 1990.
3. *Washington Post*, December 11, 1990.
4. Ibid.
5. Cited in John T. Nielsen, "Immigration and the Low-Cost Housing Crisis: The Los Angeles Area's Experience," *Population and Environment*, Volume 11, Number 2, Winter 1989.
6. U.S. General Accounting Office, *Rural Development: Problems and Progress of Colonia Subdivisions Near Mexico Border*, GAO/RCED-91-37, November 1990.
7. Edward Roybal, "National ID Card Voted Down," *National Hispanic Reporter*, Volume I, Number 4, December 1990.
8. U.S. Immigration and Naturalization Service, Statistical Division, 1990 Enforcement and Assaults Data, Washington, May 1991.
9. Dennis DeConcini, Statement Regarding the GAO Report on Border Patrol, Washington, April 3, 1991.
10. Roberto Suro, "Traffic in Fake Documents is Blamed as Illegal Immigration Rises Anew," *New York Times*, November 26, 1990.
11. Ibid.
12. *Washington Post*, "State of America: Census Report," March 3, 1991.
13. U.S. Department of Commerce, Bureau of the Census, "Census Bureau Completes Distribution of 1990 Redistricting Tabulations to States," Washington, March 11, 1991.
14. Leon Bouvier and David Simcox, *Many Hands, Few Jobs: Population, Unemployment and Emigration in Mexico and the Caribbean*, Center for Immigration Studies, Washington, 1986.

138

15. George J. Borjas and Marta Tienda, "The Economic Consequences of Immigration," *Science* 235, February 1987; as cited in U.S. Department of Labor, Bureau of International Labor Affairs, *The Effects of Immigration on the U.S. Economy and Labor Market*, Washington, December 1988.
16. Daniel James, "A Crisis Begging for Coverage," *AIM Report*, June-A, 1986.

Chapter 2

1. Daniel James, *Mexico and the Americans,* New York, Frederick A. Praeger, Inc., 1963.
2. James, *Mexico and the Americans.*
3. Henry Bamford Parkes, *A History of Mexico,* Boston, Houghton Mifflin Company, 1950.
4. National Council of La Raza, *Beyond Ellis Island: Hispanics—Immigrants and Americans,* Washington, 1986.
5. Congressional Research Service, *History of the Immigration and Naturalization Service*, Ninety-sixth Congress, Second Session, 1980.
6. Arthur F. Corwin (ed.), *Immigrants and Immigrants: Perspectives on Mexican Labor Migration to the United States*, Westport, CT, Greenwood Press, 1978.

Chapter 3

1. Coppock, Donald R., Deputy Associate Commissioner, Domestic Control, Department of Justice, *History of the Border Patrol*, Washington, probably 1976; unpublished.
2. Congressional Research Service, *History of the Immigration and Naturalization Service*, Ninety-sixth Congress, Second Session. U.S. Government Printing Office, Washington, 1980.
3. Luis Horacio Durán, *The Mexican Migration to the United States of America: Considerations of its History, and its Impact on the Culture of the United States and on the Economy of Both Nations*, Monterrey, Mexico, 1980.
4. National Council of La Raza, *Beyond Ellis Island.*
5. Bouvier and Simcox, *Many Hands, Few Jobs.*

139

6. Cited in Robert Lee Strout, "A Fence for the Rio Grande," *The Independent* , June 2, 1928.
7. Coppock, *Border Patrol.*
8. Ibid.
9. Cited in Manuel García y Griego, "The Importation of Mexican Contract Laborers to the United States, 1942-1964: Antecedents, Operation, and Legacy," in Peter G. Brown and Henry Shue (ed.), *The Border that Joins,* Totowah, NJ, Rowman and Littlefield, 198).
10. Department of Justice, Immigration and Naturalization Service, Annual Report, 1955.
11. Coppock, *Border Patrol.*
12. Michael S. Teitelbaum, *Latin Migration North: The Problem for U.S. Foreign Policy,* Washington, Council on Foreign Relations, 1985.
13. David S. North and Marion F. Houston, *Characteristics and Role of Illegal Aliens in the U. S. Labor Market: An Exploratory Study* Washington, Linton & Co., 1976.
14. Immigration and Naturalization Service, Provisional Legalization Application Statistics, August 27, 1990.
15. Francisco Alba, "The Mexican Demographic Situation," Woodlands Center for Growth Studies, 1987.
16. Bouvier and Simcox, *Many Hands, Few Jobs.*
17. United Nations, World Population Prospects, 1990.
18 International Labor Office, *Economically Active Population, 1950-2025*, Volume III, Geneva. See Francisco Javier Alejo, "Demographic Patterns and Labor Market Trends in Mexico," *Mexico's Economic Crisis: Challenges and Opportunities,* La Jolla, CA, Center for U.S. Mexican Studies, 1983.

Chapter 4

1. Emmerich de Vattel, *The Law of Nations*, 1758.
2. *Guia del Extranjero, Ley General de Población de 1979* Mexico City, Editorial Porrua, S. A., 1986.
3. Immigration and Nationality Act (as amended), Washington, U.S. Government Printing Office, 1989.
4. *Congressional Record,* March 16, 1896, 54th Congress, 1st Session.
5. *Washington Times*, May 21, 1991.

6. "Selective Service Notifies Aliens of Registration Requirement," *Interpreter Releases*, January 7, 1991.
7. Justice Thompson, *City of New York v. Miln* (36 US 102).
8. Corwin, *Mexican Labor Migration.*

Chapter 5

1. *Washington Post*, March 16, 1991.
2. Ibid.
3. M. D. Van Arsdol et al., *Non-apprehended Undocumented Residents in the Los Angeles Labor Market: An Exploratory Study,* Los Angeles, University of Southern California Press, 1979.
4. Borjas, *Wall Street Journal*, November 8, 1990.
5. Daniel Stein and Steven Zanowic, "Permanent Resident AliensUnder Color of Law: The Opening Door to Alien Entitlement Eligibility," *Georgetown Immigration Law Review*, Vol. 1, No. 2, Spring 1986.
6. David North, *Aliens and the Regular and Irregular Labor Markets*, Washington, Transcentury Development Associates, 1989.
7. *Washington Times,* May 25, 1990, "City of Angels has Hellish Tale."
8. Ibid.
9. *Washington Times,* May 21, 1990.
10. *Valley Morning Star*, November 11, 1986, "Schools in Hidalgo County Still Fighting Numbers Game."
11. *New York Daily News*, December 7, 1990.
12. County of Los Angeles, Department of Health Services, Reports of Health Services to Undocumented Aliens for Fiscal Years 1983 to 1989.
13. *San Diego Tribune*, March 19, 1990.
14. *Washington Post*, December 2, 1990.
15. Lief Jensen, "Patterns of Immigration and Public Assistance Utilization," *International Migration Review*, Vol. 22, Spring 1988.
16. Thomas Muller, Thomas J. Espenshade, et al., *The Fourth Wave: California's Newest Immigrants,* Washington, Urban Press Institute, 198).
17. David North, "Impact of Legal, Illegal and Refugee Migrations on U.S. Social Service Programs," in Mary Kritz (ed.), *U.S. Immigration and Refugee Policy*, New York: Lexington, 1982.
18. Borjas, "The U. S. Takes the Wrong Immigrants," *Wall Street Journal*, April 5, 1990.

19. Daniel James, interview, March 25, 1986.
20. Borjas, *Friends or Strangers: The Impact of Immigrants on the U.S. Economy,* New York, Basic Books, 1990.
21. Sidney Weintraub, *A Marriage of Convenience: Relations Between Mexico and the United States, a Twentieth Century Fund Report* , New York, Oxford University Press, 1990.
22. Barry R. Chiswick, "Is the New Immigration Less Skilled Than the Old?" *Journal of Labor Economics*, Vol. 4, No. 2, April 1986, University of Illinois at Chicago.

Chapter 6

1. Weintraub, *Marriage of Convenience.*
2. Ibid.
3. *The President's Comprehensive Triennial Report on Immigration,* Washington, U.S. Government Printing Office, 1989.
4. Borjas, *Wall Street Journal*, April 5, 1990.
5. Espenshade and Muller, *The Fourth Wave.*
6. E. Ray Marshall, "Immigration in the Golden State: The Tarnished Dream," cited in David E. Simcox (ed.) *U.S. Immigration in the 1980's,* Boulder CO, Westview Press, 1988.
7. Julian L. Simon, *The Economic Consequences of Immigration*, Basil Blackwell, Published in Association with the Cato Institute, London 1989.
8. Ibid.
9. Ibid.
10. Ibid.
11. Frank Morris, Statement, Hearings, House Subcommittee on Immigration, Refugees and International Law on Legal Immigration Reform, Washington, March 13, 1990.
12. Ibid.
13. Michael Powell, *New York Newsday*, January 8, 1989, cited in Center for Immigration Studies, *Scope*, Washington, Fall/Winter 1990/1991 issue.
14. Immigration and Nationality Act (as amended), U.S. Government Printing Office,Washington, 1989.
15. Paul R. Ehrlich, *The Golden Door, International Migration, Mexico, and the United States,* New York, Random House, 1979.

16. Immigration Reform and Control Act, U.S. Government Printing Office, Washington, 1986.
17. United States General Accounting Offfice, Washington, April 1990.
18. Ibid.
19. William Raspberrry, "Recipe for an Immigration Disaster," *Washington Post*, November 12, 1986.
20. Corwin, *Mexican Labor Migration.*
21. Philip Martin, *Illegal Immigration and the Colonization of the American Labor Market,* Center for Immigration Studies, Washington, 1986.
22. Marshall, "Immigration in the Golden State."

Chapter 7

1. Corwin, *Mexican Labor Migration.*
2. Daniel Wolf, *Undocumented Aliens and Crime —The Case of San Diego County,* San Diego, University of California Press, 1988.
3. Edd Clark, "Historic Texas Town Fertile Ground for Border Bandits," *Valley Morning Star*, November 15, 1986.
4. Gail Diane Cox, "INS Estimates Undocumented Are One-Fifth of Jail Inmates," *Los Angeles Daily Journal*, June 20, 1986.
5. Jerry Seper, "America's Border War," *Washington Times*, May 25, 1990.
6. Ibid.
7. U.S. General Accounting Office, *Border Patrol, Southwest Border Enforcement Affected by Mission Expansion and Budget*, Washington, March 1991.
8. Seper, " America's Border War."

Chapter 8

1. United States State Department, Bureau of International Narcotics Matters, *International Narcotics Control Strategy Report*, Washington, March 1991.
2. Alan C. Nelson, Statement before the House Subcommittee on Crime, Washington, May 22, 1986.
3. *Washington Post,* April 21, 1986.

4. William von Raab, Hearings, Western Hemisphere Affairs Subcommittee, Foreign Relations Committee, United States Senate, May 13, 1986.
5. Ibid.
6. *Washington Post*, April 21, 1986.
7. *Washington Post*, February 2 and February 4, 1991.
8. Bureau of International Narcotics Matters, *Narcotics Control Report.*
9. Ibid.
10. Ibid.
11. Javier Livas, "The Mexican Narcopolitical System," *Mexico-United States Report*, June 1990.
12. Ibid.
13. Ibid.
14. Terrence E. Poppa, *Druglord — the Life and Death of a Mexican Kingpin,* New York, Pharos Books, 1990.
15. Ibid.
16. Livas, "Mexican Narcopolitical System."
17. Ibid.
18 Ibid.
19. Bureau of International Narcotics Matters, *Narcotics Control Report.*
20. Peter Ronstadt, Statement before the Senate Subcommittee on Treasury, Postal Service and General Government, Committee on Appropriations, Tucson, Arizona, June 28, 1989.
21. Michael Huckaby, ibid.
22. Samuel T. Francis, *Illegal Immigration— A Threat to U.S. Security,* London, Centre for Security and Conflict Studies, 1986.

Chapter 9

1. *Washington Post*, May 12, 1991.
2. *New York Times*, May 8, 1991.
3. *Washinton Post*, May 7, 1991.
4. *New York Times*, May 8, 1991.
5. *Washington Post*, May 9, 1991.
6. *Washington Post*, May 12, 1991.
7. *Washington Post*, May 7, 1991.
8. *Washington Post*, May 13, 1991.

9. Telephone interview, May 16, 1991.
10. CBS, "Face the Nation," May 13, 1991.
11. *New York Times*, May 8, 1991.
12 *Washington Post*, May 10, 1991.
13. Ibid.
14. *Washington Post*, May 12, 1991
15. Robert J. Thomas, "Citizenship, Gender and Work," *Social Organization in Industrial Agriculture,* Berkeley, CA, University of California Press, 1985.
16. Melvin L. Oliver and James H. Johnson, Jr., "Inter-Ethnic Conflict in An Urban Ghetto: The Case of Blacks and Latinos in Los Angeles," *Research in Social Movements, Conflict and Change,* Vol. 6, 1984.
17. Morris, Hearings, Immigration, Refugees and International Law.
18. Juan Williams, "Black Power's New Dilemma," *Outlook, Washington Post,* May 13, 1991.
19. Raúl Yzaguirre, Statement, 40th Anniversary Annual Dinner, National Council of La Raza, May 8, 1990.
20. Ibid.
21. Linda Chavez, "Rainbow Collision—The Hispanic-Black Feud, *New Republic*, November 19, 1990.
22. Joel Kotkin, "Black Economic Base in L.A. Erodes as Demographics Change," *Washington Post*, October 1, 1989.

Chapter 10

1. Georges Fauriol, "U.S. Immigration Policy and the National Interest," *The Humanist*, May/June, 1984.
2. William A. Henry III, *Time,* June 13, 1983. Cited in Fauriol.
3. Ysidro Ramón Macías, "The Chicano Movement, " *Wilson Library Bulletin*, March, 1970.
4. R.E. Butler, *On Creating A Hispanic America: A Nation Within A Nation?*, Council for Inter-American Security, Washington, 1985.
5. Cited in Butler, ibid.
6. Rodolfo González, "What Political Road for the Chicano Movement?", *The Militant*, March 30, 1970.
7. Corwin, *Mexican Labor Migration.*
8. Kevin McCarthy and R. Burciaga Valdez, *Current and Future Effects of Mexican Immigration in California,* Santa Monica, CA, RAND, 1985.

9. Georges Vernez and David Ronfeldt, "The Current Situation in Mexican Immigration," *Science*, March 8, 1991.
10. General Accounting Office, *The Future Flow of Legal Immiration to the United States,* Washington, 1988.
11. Gerda Bikales and Gary Imhof, "A Kind of Discordant Harmony: Issues in Assimilation," in David E. Simcox (ed.), *Immigration in the 1980's: Reappraisal and Reform,* Boulder, CO, Westview, 1988.
12. Vernez and Ronfelt, op. cit.
13. National Council of La Raza, *Unfinished Business.*
14. Ibid.

Chapter 11

1. Amitai Etzioni, "America is Unsecured," *Washington Post*, December 11, 1985.
2. Oscar J. Martínez, *Troublesome Border*, Tucson, AZ, University of Arizona Press, 1988.
3. Samuel T. Francis, *Threat to U.S. Security.*
4. Ibid.
5. Carlyle Murphy, "FBI Suspects are Libyan Spies," *Washington Post*, July 23, 1988.
6. Bill Gertz, "Khomeini Henchmen Lurk Here, FBI Says," *Washington TImes*, March 9, 1989.
7. Charles Phillips, "Meltdown of the Melting Pot," *American Legion*, Vol. 127, No. 2, August,1989.
8. Daniel James, interview, March 27, 1986.
9. Ibid.

Chapter 12

1. Bouvier and Simcox, *Many Hands, Few Jobs.*
2. Seth Mydans, "More Mexicans Come to the U.S. to Stay," *New York Times*, January 21, 1991.
3. Luis Horacio Durán, *Mexican Migration to the United States.*
4. Frank D. Bean, Barry Edmontson and Jeffrey Pessel, *Undocumented Migration to the United States: IRCA and the Experience of the 1980s,* Washington, Urban Institute, 1990.

5. Lawrence Cardoso, *Mexican Emigration to the United States, 1897-1931: Socio-Economic Patterns*, Tucson, AZ, Arizona University Press, 1980.
6. Report of the Commission for the Study of International Migration.
7. Ibid.
8. *New York Times,* April 9, 1991.
9. Steven García, President, National Border Patrol Council, AFL-CIO, Testimony Before the Sub-Committee on Human Rights, Committee on Foreign Affairs, U.S. House of Representatives, April 18, 1990.
10. Federation for American Immigration Reform, *Ten Steps to Securing America's Borders*, Washington, 1989.

What is the Mexico-United States Institute?

THE MEXICO-UNITED STATES INSTITUTE was founded in January, 1987, by a group of Americans and Mexicans who decided it was high time to focus public attention on the worsening crisis in Mexico, and on its potentially grave consequences both for that country and the United States. It was also time, they felt, that the two neighbors set an agenda for the 1990s and beyond, based upon the realities of their respective societies.

If the central aim of MUSI can be summed up in a phrase, it is: *democracy must get ahead of the curve of history.* We need "democracy without adjectives," as the Mexican political scientist, Enrique Krause, has put it, if humanity is to achieve representative government and freedom.

Economic freedom goes hand in hand with political freedom. Thus MUSI has steadfastly advocated the privatization of Mexico's statist economy along with the democratization of its political system, while it called upon President George Bush to work for a North American Free Trade Agreement as soon he was elected in November 1988.

The Mexican crisis, though much attenuated by the serious economic reforms of President Carlos Salinas de Gortari, nevertheless remains troubling. But few Americans seem aware of it. At any rate, until MUSI there was no major off-campus public or private institution in the United States that was binational in scope and was dedicated exclusively, or even in some substantial measure, to the task of addressing a problem so profoundly important to both neighbors.

MUSI's fundamental purpose is clear and simple: to study, research and analyze U. S.-Mexican relations *exclusively*, in all their ramifications, *on a continuing basis*. In furtherance of that purpose, it strives to observe the highest academic standards and strictest adherence to the facts while making its own analyses and interpretations of them.

Though independent of government, MUSI is not a "think-tank" divorced from the realities of power in Mexico City and Washington. Rather, it aims to influence the decision-making process through an ongoing effort to educate and inform. Its labors are meant to foster not just "closer," but truly *informed*, bilateral relations on all levels—cultural, historical and human as well as social, economic and political—so that both neighbors may live together in peace, prosperity and freedom.

The Mexico-United States Institute is chartered in the District of Columbia. It is a privately supported nonprofit organization which is tax exempt under Section 501(c) (3) of the Internal Revenue Code.

About the Author

DANIEL JAMES, President and Chief Executive Officer of the Mexico-United States Institute, has specialized in Latin American affairs for more than thirty years, with particular emphasis on Mexico. He lived in Mexico for over two decades, working as an author and journalist.

He has published three books on that country, *Mexico and the Americans, How to Live and Invest in Mexico,* and *Where Mexico Stands.* He has also authored four other books including *Cuba: First Soviet Satellite in the Americas* and *Che Guevara, a Biography.*

Numerous shorter works and articles on Mexico and other Latin American countries by the author have appeared in such diverse publications as *Fortune, Harper's, London Observer Colour Magazine, New York Times Magazine, Reader's Digest, Washington Quarterly, Boston Globe, Chicago Tribune, Houston Chronicle, Washington Post,* and *Washington Times.*

He has conducted or collaborated in studies on Mexico and other Latin American countries sponsored by the Twentieth Century Fund of New York, Foreign Policy Research Institute of Philadelphia, and the Hudson Institute. He served as Adjunct Fellow of the Center for Strategic and International Studies, in a project on Mexico in crisis.

Daniel James holds a doctorate in Latin American Studies and a B.A. in Journalism.

Mexico-United States Institute
1910 K Street, N.W., Suite 402
Washington, D.C. 20006
(202)775-8560

Index

154

Immigration

- Selecting Mexico → USA

Legislation Governing it

Why migrate north - economic conditions there
—.—————→ USA

Effect - legal
       + illegal migrant has on

       US workers
       US economy

What's done to prevent illegal immigrants